THE GERMAN-SPEAKING FORTY-EIGHTERS:

Builders of Watertown, Wisconsin

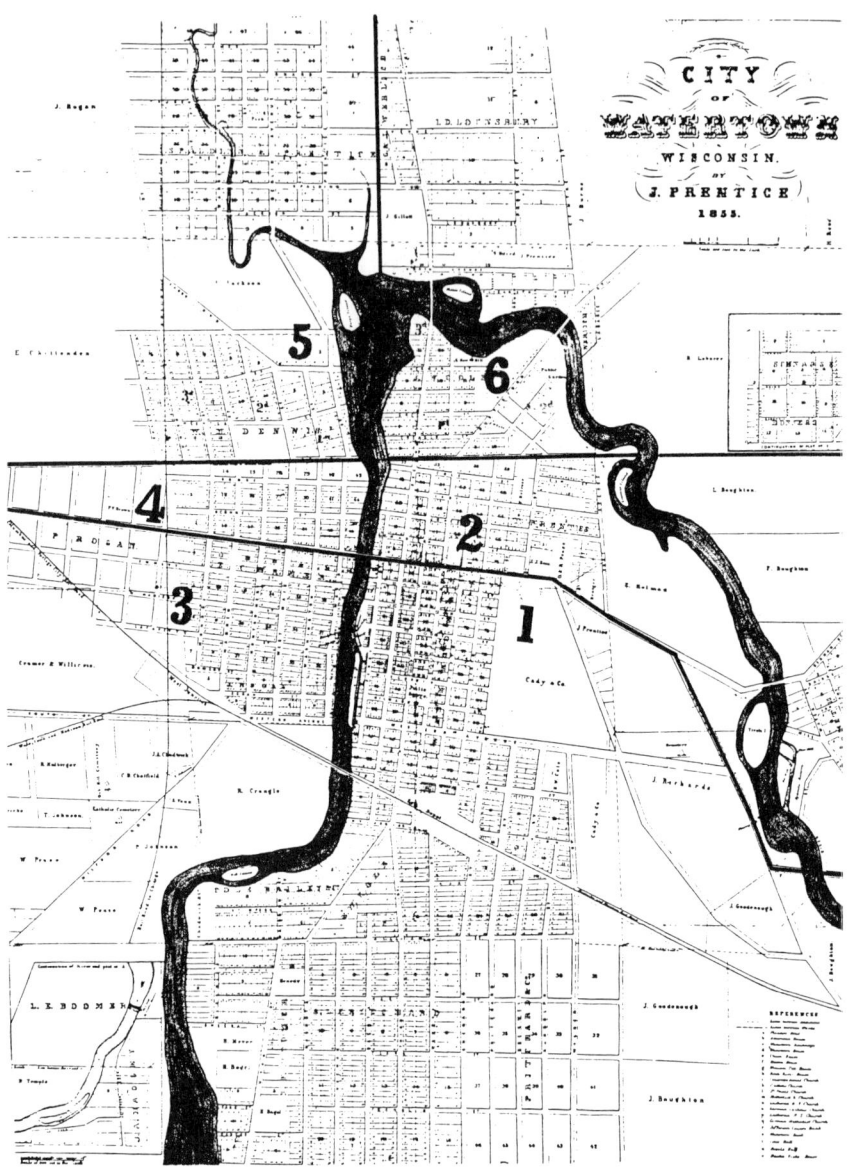

Watertown — 1855

This 1855 map of Watertown shows the location of its various wards. The Rock River divides the east wards from those on the west side. The main street traverses the city from east to west at a slight angle.

THE GERMAN-SPEAKING FORTY-EIGHTERS:

Builders of Watertown, Wisconsin

Charles J. Wallman

The Max Kade Institute for German-American Studies
University of Wisconsin-Madison
Madison, Wisconsin

This narrative is dedicated to my wife, Chee Chee, in appreciation of her understanding and patience during the two years it was being compiled and written.

PREFACE

The year 1848 was marked by revolutionary uprisings all over Europe: France overthrew the Bourbons; Poland struggled against Russia; some Italian states rebelled against the Austrian overlords as well as against territorial domination by the Pope; insurgent movements broke out in Hungary. In the 35 German states ruled by princes, and in the Empire of Austria-Hungary, citizens of all classes aired their grievances.

The cries for "Freedom" and "Unity" were heard again. They had first inspired the American, and then the French revolutionaries; they had been repeated in the Wars of Liberation against Napoleon; they had been suppressed again after Napoleon's defeat by the Holy Alliance of Russia, Austria, and the German States.

In March of 1848, almost all the German rulers felt the displeasure of their citizens. They demonstrated, they marched, they went on the barricades. As a consequence, ministers were dismissed and princes abdicated. But that was not enough.

Elected representatives of the people meeting in St. Paul's Church in Frankfurt established the Frankfurt Parliament. Their assembly gathered under the black-red-gold colours of liberalism; it drafted a bill of human rights and a constitution for all of Germany (from which, however, Austria was excluded). Some of the more radical Forty-Eighters hoped that their dream of a German republic might soon be realized; the majority of the delegates, however, wanted a unified Germany under a constitutional monarch. They offered the imperial crown to the King of Prussia who refused to take the sacred symbol from the hands of the people.

Within a year the dream of German unity and a constitutional monarchy was over. Lacking financial power, without a central coordinating authority, and without sustained military strength, the uprisings all over Europe were crushed by the fall of 1849. In Germany, Austria, Hungary, Italy, Poland, and France the reaction was swift and merciless. Whoever had taken part in the demonstrations could expect expulsion from school or the university, or dismissal from work. Fines, loss of property, jail, and even death punished those who had taken an active part in the uprisings.

Unless, of course, they had managed to flee the country. Thus it is that we meet descendents of the Forty-Eighters in England, in Switzerland, in South America, and in the United States. About 70,000 people, it is estimated, fled from the German-speaking countries to the U. S. because they had experienced, or feared, reprisals for their participation in the revolts of 1848-49. Many more citizens decided that this was a good time to leave a European continent where political and economic conditions were bound to be stagnant for years to come.

The Max Kade Institute for German-American Studies at the University of Wisconsin in Madison is dedicated to researching the contributions of German-speaking immigrants to the United States. The contributions to the social, political, and cultural life of the United States by the Forty-Eighters were the topic of a symposium sponsored by the Institute in 1986. These essays have been collected in the volume "The German-speaking Forty-Eighters in the United States" published by Peter Lang, Berne-New York, 1989.

Mr. Charles J. Wallman, a life-long resident of Watertown, Wisconsin, took part in the Forty-Eighter symposium. He has identified more than sixty of these Forty-Eighters who settled in Watertown, then the second-largest city in Wisconsin. Most of them came from the German-speaking countries, but there were also individuals from Poland, Hungary, France, Denmark, i.e. Schleswig-Holstein. There were the "rebels and revolutionaries," but also several immigrants who had supported their various governments during the years 1848-49. Some Forty-Eighter families stayed for a short time, others can still be recognized in their present-day descendents.

Today, when so many people are retracing their roots by working seriously on their genealogical tables, the work done by Mr. Wallman should be considered exemplary. By consulting the source materials in English and German he has skillfully unravelled the threads that tie the Forty-Eighters and their descendents to the history of Watertown; he has chronicled not only the Forty-Eighters who subsequently became prominent in the German-American community of the United States but also those who never moved again and helped make their new hometown a thriving place. He has shown that energy and industry, the love of intellectual and cultural life, and the capacity for friendship were outstanding traits of the Forty-Eighter families.

Mr. Wallman's book and pictures are an indispensable guide for anyone who wants to understand the past and the present of the Watertown community.

> Charlotte Lang Brancaforte,
> Professor of German
> Director, Max Kade Institute for
> German-American Studies

December 10, 1989

Contents

List of Illustrations

NOTE: All of the illustrations in this book have come from the files of the Watertown Historical Society, with the following exceptions. Those on pages 30, 78, and 79 were furnished by Rev. Max Gaebler. The illustrations on pages 57 and 58 have been supplied by Margaret Salick Luchsinger. Catherine Jean Quirk provided the portrait on page 68. The map of the City of Watertown appearing as the frontispiece was drawn by Judson Prentiss in 1855. Andrew M. Wallman took the original pictures on pages 59, 63, and 70.

Introduction & Acknowledgements

Early in 1986, the Max Kade Institute for German-American Studies at the University of Wisconsin-Madison issued a "Call for Papers" to scholars and students of history to submit papers for a symposium on "the Forty-Eighters" to be held at the university in the fall of that same year. The papers themselves were to deal specifically with "the contribution of German-speaking immigrants to the USA whose coming was directly related to their involvement in the events connected with the Revolution of 1848-49." The call further stipulated that the papers were to deal with "the contributions of such immigrants to the social, political and cultural life of the USA."

This narrative is an expansion of a paper accepted for presentation at that symposium and deals with the Forty-Eighters who came to Watertown, Wisconsin. It relates to individuals who were involved in the Revolution, both as dissidents and as counter-revolutionaries who remained loyal to the government.

My deepest appreciation to Charlotte Lang Brancaforte, professor of German and director of the Max Kade Institute, and to Theodore Hamerow, professor of history at UW-Madison for their encouragement and for their confidence in asking me to expand that paper into this much longer format.

I'm particularly appreciative of the fine foreword by Professor Brancaforte. She has been a continuing source of enthusiasm in regard to this narrative, and for that I'm extremely grateful. My thanks also to Professor Hamerow for his assistance in working out one of the particularly difficult portions of this story.

Further, I'm very grateful to the Watertown Historical Society for the use of many of the pictures that appear in this book. In addition, Rev. Max Gaebler, Margaret Salick Luchsinger and the late Catherine Jean Quirk were helpful in making several of their personal photos available for inclusion.

All of the photographic work for this volume was done by my son, Andrew M. Wallman. He was able to bring to life faded, or indistinct, or extremely small pictures.

Special thanks must be extended to Kurt Busch, Creative Director of Knupp & Watson, Advertising & Marketing, Madison, for his contributions in developing the book's cover.

I am also indebted to Dr. Catherine Rasmussen for her helpful editorial work and suggestions. A valuable source on many occasions was Susanne Feller, assistant to the Director of the Max Kade Institute. Additionally, aid was given that was most useful by Dr. Arnold Lehmann, professor emeritus of Northwestern College, Watertown; Judge Arnold Schumann, trustee of Northwestern College; Maureen Hady, director of the Watertown Public Library, and her entire staff; Judy Quam, custodian of the Watertown Historical Society; Reuben Feld, local historian; and William Jannke III, president of the Watertown Genealogical Society.

This publication would not have been possible without the financial assistance of the Consulate General of Federal Republic of West Germany, Chicago; the German-American Cultural Society, Inc., Madison; and the Max Kade Institute for German-American Studies at UW-Madison. To each of them, my sincere gratitude.

Charles J. Wallman

Watertown, Wisconsin
November 30, 1989

The German-Speaking Forty-Eighters: Builders of Watertown, Wisconsin

On the night of May 10, 1848, the village of Watertown in the Wisconsin Territory buzzed with excitement. Four hundred people — townspeople and farmers, Americans and Germans alike — crowded into or around the English Methodist Church to celebrate a very special occasion, the Revolution in Germany. Since this was an extraordinary event, the church was "profusely decorated" with evergreens and garlands of prairie flowers, and with the "old German national colors (black, red and gold) and the American stars and stripes."

The proceedings were conducted by the local *Sängerverein*, known as the *Liedertafel*, which was the first singing society formed in the state. Two speeches in German and one in English stressed the theme of liberty or freedom.

The *Liedertafel*, performing the very first German concert in the community, entertained the assembly "for an hour or two." When the chorus burst forth with the "Tailor Song," the Americans in the audience joined in round after round of applause. They thought the rendition was the German national anthem and wished to show their support for the Revolution in that way. Their enthusiasm stirred the crowd into feverish excitement that subsided only after several benches holding spectators collapsed. A number of the crowd had stood on them to have a better view of the proceedings.

After the concert, a torchlight parade led by marshals wearing imposing black, red, and gold sashes marched west along Main Street across the bridge to the Liberty pole. The marchers circled the pole and sang the "Hero's Song." The procession then reformed and paraded back across the river to one of the village's leading hotels, the Buena Vista House, whose name was not pronounced locally in a Spanish or Mexican manner, but was "Byoona VISSTA."

The hotel itself was embellished with decorations in black, red and gold in keeping with the theme of the evening. The torches (and the fuel for them) as well as all of the decorative material, including

1

the marshal's sashes, had been furnished by the owners of a local retail establishment called the German Store. A "delicious supper" was served to 100 or so of the celebrants and took an hour and a half to consume. Wine was served with the meal, apparently something of a rarity in this frontier community, and many patriotic toasts were proposed.

Dancing began at midnight in the ballroom where waltzes, the cotillion, and the ecossaise were performed. From time to time the night air was punctuated by enthusiastic "salutes" from various types of weapons. The entire demonstration, the first "mass meeting" in the history of Watertown, ended at 6 o'clock the next morning. In reporting the event, one local English-language newspaper, the *Chronicle*, observed that the entire celebration "reflected equal honor upon the heads and hearts of our German fellow-citizens."

Early Watertown

Watertown's first permanent white settler arrived in 1836. The settlement was situated at a huge ox-bow bend in the Rock River called Ka-Ka-Ree by the neighboring Indians. A French fur trader had earlier lived at the site, but was murdered by the Indians in

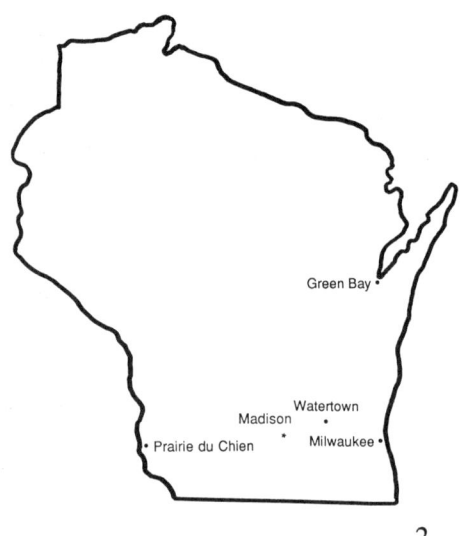

Green Bay

Watertown
Madison
Prairie du Chien   Milwaukee

Where is Watertown?

Watertown is located in southeast Wisconsin, midway between the state's largest city, Milwaukee, and the state capitol, Madison.

1827. It is unclear whether his death was caused by drunken Indians or whether it was the result of some imagined wrong.

The first German, Jacob Wiedemann, arrived in Watertown in 1837. While Yankees and Irish comprised most of the original settlers, five more Germans had arrived by 1843. Beginning in 1845, immigration into Watertown and the surrounding area was dominated by the Germans. Ebenezer Cole, one of the village's first arrivals and a Yankee, was later to observe that the survival of the settlement was "due to the money of the Germans, their iron will and their strenuous work."

The early and mid-1850s were a period of exceptional growth for Watertown. As the heart of a developing agriculture area and a major trade center, it attracted farmers from the north and west particularly who brought their products and livestock to Watertown. There they received Milwaukee prices which were higher. The huge drop in the water level in the Rock River — it was almost thirty feet — attracted a number of industrial operations. There were five

Watertown — 1842

Only six years after the village was founded, Watertown in 1842 consisted of less than a dozen small frame buildings.

3

sawmills, three flouring (or grist) mills, an iron foundry, and a woolen mill. During this same period, three railroads were either connected to Watertown or were in the process of reaching it.

By 1853, the village had become a city and was the second largest community in the state, with a population of 4,000. Of this number, 2,000 were "Germans," that is, persons from territories and lands where the German language was spoken, and which approximated the later German Empire and Austria.

German Settlement of Watertown

Germans particularly found this bustling young settlement to their liking. By 1856 every train brought two or three new families. During one period of about ten days that year, 800 of these newcomers arrived in the community. First, 300 "Prussians" arrived; they were followed by 500 more several days later. "Prussian" was a term frequently applied by both the local citizenry and a local newspaper to former inhabitants of the Kingdom of Prussia, and to North Germans in general. These newcomers were considered by their neighbors to be a healthy, intelligent people "who would make good citizens." A number brought sizable amounts of money with them.

Many of these new immigrants, probably single men, stayed at the popular Rock River House in the heart of the city, next to the river. The proprietor frequently had so many guests to accommodate that he would assign two or three persons to sleep in the same bed, a not infrequent practice in growing frontier communities.

Perhaps the most important local gathering-point for new Germans was the Hermann Meyer, farm near the northern edge of the city, in the Town of Emmet. The place attracted a mixture of former government officials, students, military officers, noblemen, merchants, artists, and others who remained until they could find their own housing and employment.

The German population of Watertown continued to grow steadily. Their presence became so dominant that in deference to some of their non-Teutonic patrons, several store owners placed signs in their display windows reading "English spoken here."

The penetration of the Germans in the city's Sixth Ward was particularly strong; this section of town was called "Little Germany," although the name could equally have been applied to the Fifth Ward. The Sixth Ward was entirely German except for two American and four Irish families, and in these years of Watertown's dynamic growth, was a leader in building. During the six months of 1855 beginning with February, for example, fifty-three new houses were erected. This was roughly one new house being completed every third work day. And each new home housed at least one family; some had three.

Watertown had a flourishing brick business at this point. Many of the newcomers used brick to build their homes, although most were decidedly small. These very tiny dwellings entered the town's vocabulary as "cracker-boxes."

The reasons that so many people left Germany for a new life in the United States — and especially to Watertown — are multiple.

Cracker box house

Many first homes of Watertown's settlers were small brick structures such as this. People in the community unaffectionately called them "cracker boxes."

Religious freedom was certainly a compelling force; both the early and the latter-day prominence of German-language churches in the Watertown community amply bear this out. Political freedom, a tenet of particular importance to many who fled following the Revolution of 1848, was very much a determinant. Near-serfdom under high-handed *Junkers* and other landowners, a stifling bureaucracy, and unreasonable taxes contributed to the process as well, as did the custom in some parts of Germany of dividing farm land among numerous offspring so that ultimately the land could not feed its owners.

The most compelling attraction of Watertown for Germans arriving in the United States was probably the presence of other Germans. A common language and culture, many common goals, and a climate and geography much like that back in *die Heimat* (the

West Avenue about 1848

This portion of Watertown's main street extending west from the Main Street bridge was called West Avenue. This is the earliest known street scene photographed within the village. The building at the right is the Rock River House, a popular stopping place for arriving immigrants.

homeland) were considerations of importance. It was a perception of "German-ness" or *Deutschtum*, together with the expectation of limitless opportunity, that drew the Forty-Eighters to Watertown, Wisconsin, which by 1856 boasted a population of 10,006 in the city and township combined.

The first Forty-Eighter to arrive in Watertown seems to have been a former student from Heidelberg University by the name of Schumann. Except for his last name and the name of his university, nothing is known about him. Ralph D. Blumenfeld, a long-time newspaperman with impeccable credentials and son of Forty-Eighter David Blumenfeld, wrote that "a dozen or more" of the Forty-Eighter element came to Watertown. By searching newspapers, church records, family files, and interviewing present-day family members, I have been able to identify sixty-one Forty-Eighters in the community.

The typical Watertown Forty-Eighter was a man from western or southwestern Germany, about twenty-nine years of age at the time of the Revolution. He moved to the United States in 1848 or 1849 and came directly to Watertown. If he did not come directly to the city, he had worked his way slowly westward and arrived in 1855. The Forty-Eighter generally had no formal religious affiliation; the majority of those who adhered to a religious philosophy belonged to the local *Freie Gemeinde*. A scattering were either Lutheran or Catholic. The typical Forty-Eighter married and had about five children. Because he had a "good" education (frequently at the university level), he was either involved in intellectual pursuits, or was a tradesman or craftsman. He became involved in politics, primarily within the city. Our Forty-Eighter was generally a Democrat who spent the remainder of his life in Watertown and died near the age of seventy-eight.

The Latin Farmers

The need for food and shelter for themselves and their families forced hard, realistic choices on many of these immigrants, few of whom spoke English. They had to accept whatever work they could find where language was not a factor.

About a dozen of this group, all painfully ignorant of agricultural methods, experimented with farming. Generally it was intellectuals who made this choice; the artisans and craftsmen had their trades which they could continue to follow. Since most of these would-be farmers had a university education, they were laughingly called the *Lateinische Farmer* (Latin farmers) or in good German on occasion, *Lateinische Bauern* (Latin peasants). The latter title may have been a phrase peculiar to the Watertown area.

A Latin farmer of Watertown was once seen tilling his field, his horse-drawn plow in one hand, a copy of Virgil's *Georgics* in Latin in the other. Since the *Georgics* deals with agriculture and related subjects, one has to wonder if the old revolutionary was trying to become a Wisconsin farmer by reading of farming methods which Virgil had described 1,900 years earlier. What a sight this misguided immigrant must have presented as he stumbled over clods of dirt, trying to guide both his horse and plow while reviewing the heady material he had studied as a youth in school.

Another academic émigré-turned-farmer was closely watched by his wife as he sowed wheat for the first time. Though she herself lacked farming experience, she realized that her husband wasn't sowing enough grain to produce a good crop. Yet she didn't wish to offend him by telling him that he was not doing the job properly. After her exhausted husband had fallen asleep at night, the helpful wife stole out into the fields and sowed more grain by hand.

Charles M. Ducasse had been a civil engineer engaged in road building in Hesse Darmstadt at the time of the Revolution. He came to Watertown and promptly became a farmer. Ducasse, called "Squire" by his neighbors, was more enterprising than most of his fellow Latin farmers. He decided to make beer to supplement his very modest farm income.

When a batch of his brew was ready for sale, the Squire mounted his snow-white horse and, followed by an ox-drawn cart carrying the precious cargo, rode slowly into Watertown. There he called on one saloon after another, trying to sell his uninspired beer. Sales were generally not too brisk; it was reported that his brew was so dark "that it [would have been] impossible to recognize a frog had one been in a glass of [Ducasse's] beer."

When these ambitious forays failed, Ducasse returned to his farm and, rather than waste the nutritious elements within the barrels, fed the undrinkable mixture to his hogs. The swine could later be seen lying on their backs squealing, while pawing the air with their feet. This display told the entire community that another of the Squire's beer-making efforts had gone astray. The Squire (whose name, Ducasse, was pronounced locally as "dickasay") eventually abandoned farming and moved into the city to follow other pursuits.

Among the few who succeeded at farming were Paul Creydt, once a professor of chemistry, Hermann H. Winter, a philologist and theologian who had taught at the University of Bonn, and Baron Hugo von Bredow, a nobleman and former cavalry officer. Ignatz Jahna, who farmed northwest of the city near Richwood for thirty-two years, had been born in Austria and served in the military

Pioneer cabin

This log cabin located several miles east of the city was the home of early settlers Friedrich and Johanna Schumacher. The cabin, largely expanded and totally enclosed, still remains standing.

for twenty-one years, including his participation in the siege of the fortress Komorn in Hungary during the Revolution.

The only Watertown Forty-Eighter with any previous exposure to farming was Frederick Brandt whose father had been a *colonus*. A *colonus*, while theoretically a free person, was required to stay on the land where he was born and was not permitted to move away. He paid ground-rent to the landowner as well as furnishing him with produce. Brandt, however, defied the obligation to stay where he was born and left home at such an early age that it is unlikely he had acquired any real knowledge of agriculture methods. He never followed any farming pursuits during his lifetime.

Henry Colonius, a Forty-Eighter who wrote the first comprehensive history of Watertown, described the efforts of the local "Latin Farmers" in this way — "the year 1848, with its revolu-

Wiggenhorn's cigarmakers

The Wiggenhorn cigar-making "manufactory" was the largest such operation in Watertown. Note the relative youth of most of the workers — few had whiskers. The familiar Wiggenhorn gilded Indian is part of the group.

tionary movements in Europe, increased the migration to America, especially in Germany. Many so-called Latin farmers particularly came in that year. Their assimilation into other fields where they could use their education is to be regarded more as an interjection brought about by the memory of 1848, and has little to do with the history of Watertown."

The Cigarmakers

One possible livelihood for new arrivals with limited finances was cigarmaking, which required a relatively modest investment. The first cigarmakers of Watertown were Theodore Bernhard and Emil Rothe. They were later considered to have founded the cigar industry of Wisconsin. They had a small bachelor's apartment at Jacob Karst's saloon and there turned out hand-cut smoking tobacco as well as cigars. They used tobacco grown in Pennsylvania and Cuba. Their products were known for excellent quality as well as their exceptionally low prices.

Rothe and Bernhard had to take payment for their fine products in a most unusual way, presumably from their landlord, Karst. They received half the price of their cigars in drinks while the other half was carried on their books for an indefinite period. They didn't become rich through this arrangement and, as a result, had to find other work.

Another who turned his hands to cigarmaking was Ernst Grossmann, once a student of medicine at the University of Gießen and later a postmaster in Hesse Darmstadt. He located in Fischer's block, a so-called German "bazaar" that in actuality was a hodgepodge of small shops within a frame building perched on stilts or pilings at the Main Street bridge in the middle of the Rock River. Grossman's brother, Carl worked with him for a time.

Although he did not make cigars himself, William Wiggenhorn encouraged two of his sons in that undertaking. They did so as a part-time endeavor when they were not otherwise occupied in the Buena Vista House owned by their father. The cigar business expanded slowly, eventually occupying a large, beautiful, three-story building on West Avenue (now West Main Street). Wiggenhorn Brothers employed as many as fifty people at one time, many of them beardless youths. The operation turned out more than three million cigars yearly and became the second largest cigar manufacturer in Wisconsin. The business prospered, and eventually a subsidiary was opened in Montana.

Mine Host

The father of the Wiggenhorn entrepreneurs was the senior Forty-Eighter in Watertown. William Wiggenhorn was fifty-one years old when he arrived in the city in 1848. Previously he had been a merchant as well as the postmaster of Schöppingen, Westphalia. He brought with him his wife and eight children, some of whom were adults.

Wiggenhorn's cigar factory

Wiggenhorn's cigar factory, with its gilded Indian, is the background for a group of singers who came to the *Sängerfest*. The signs greet them "long live the violin and the flute, long live [the poets] Schiller and Goethe,"—"welcome brothers, united in songs,"—"the consumption of cigars shows culture..."

After searching for a suitable means of earning a livelihood, Wiggenhorn purchased the partially-completed Buena Vista House at the northwest corner of North Fourth and Jones Streets. He was so eager to start his new life that he opened his hotel for business before all the walls had been plastered.

The Buena Vista quickly acquired an outstanding reputation, due in part to its good lodging and in part to Wiggenhorn's reputation as a gracious host. Equally important was the excellent food it served, prepared by his wife, Josephine, who was affectionately known to the traveling public as "Grandmama" Wiggenhorn and who at one time had fifty grandchildren. Within four short years of its opening, one observer noted that "the only excellent German hotels in the West are Wettstein's in Milwaukie [sic] and the Buena Vista in Watertown."

Fachwerk barn
The timber-and-masonry construction *(Fachwerk)* so often seen in Europe was rarely used in and around Watertown. This barn which is east of the city is the only remaining example in the local area. The builder's family lived in a plastered portion of the barn for a number of years.

13

The Baron von Bredow was also an innkeeper for a time. He operated the Boston House at the western terminus of the Watertown Plank Road (today known as Oconomowoc Avenue). When the fifty-eight mile long Plank Road was completed in 1853, it was the longest in the state and it quickly became the most profitable, for it linked the two largest cities in Wisconsin and was heavily traveled. The thoroughfare was also known by some as the Milwaukee Plank Road.

On one occasion von Bredow placed an ad in the local German newspaper inviting the populace to come to his hotel on the following Sunday afternoon for music, dancing, and as a special event, to witness a cockfight. In the excitement of making arrangements for everything that was to happen, the absent-minded Baron forgot to announce in his ad the time that the main event of the big day was to occur.

Von Bredow also owned at one time a small inn about four miles east of the city along the Plank Road route between Watertown and Ixonia.

The Plank Road name remains alive and well today as the Watertown Plank Road, a main east-west thoroughfare in Milwaukee.

When the enterprising Squire Ducasse moved into town, he took over the operation of the *Schweizer Haus* located on Main Street, between Fourth and Fifth. It was a popular stopping place for immigrants, and, in contrast to his farming and brewing efforts, became profitable for Ducasse.

The *Schuetzenhof* operated by Adolf Beurhaus was also located on Main Street between Second and Third. Beurhaus's life came to an abrupt end in September 1861 when the pistol he was cleaning accidentally discharged. The shot went through his heart and he died instantly.

An occasional reminder of the Revolution to local residents was the Kossuth House at the southeast corner of Main Street and College Avenue. It had been named after Louis Kossuth, the fiery leader of the Revolution in Hungary. Admiration for Kossuth, and the influence the Forty-Eighters had achieved within Watertown, became apparent when Kossuth Street was created in the early 1890s in the southeast part of the city. The street was located in the heart of the an area populated by a small group of German-speaking immigrants from Bohemia. In contrast, it was not until 1955 that Carl Schurz Drive was created.

Saloons and Distilleries

While operating a hotel proved manageable for some of these new German arrivals, the opening of a saloon was less demanding. Beer drinking was a well-established part of the German tradition, while lager beer was considered locally as "a healthy drink, and a medicine for body and soul."

As Watertown grew, it was quickly dotted with saloons, a number of them conducted by Forty-Eighters. By 1877 the city had seventy-three such establishments which the *Watertown Weltbürger* pointed out was a ratio of one saloon for every 137 persons. If the average family of that time consisted of five persons (husband, wife, three children), and recognizing that women and children didn't patronize saloons, this meant that twenty-seven Watertown men supported each such establishment. This condition indicates a healthy consumption of the golden brew by male Watertownians.

A local newspaperman compiled a small promotional booklet in 1856 at the request of the city council, touting the many advantages of Watertown and urging businesses and individuals to locate there. The material was directed primarily toward "our eastern friends" whom the author may have perceived as being of a staid Puritan background. While listing the dozens of business enterprises that flourished in Watertown, the author conveniently forgot to make any mention of its saloon population.

One of the early Forty-Eighter saloon proprietors was Henry Bieber, once a theology and philology student at the University of Erlangen, and a man deeply committed to the Revolution. His stint as a saloonkeeper was short, and he went on to other endeavors, including packing cigars in the Wiggenhorn cigar factory.

Jacob Karst who farmed for a time north of Watertown, came to the city and opened *Zum Freischütz* near the northeast corner of

Second and Main. His partner for a time was the unfortunate Adolph Beurhaus.

Karst's saloon was especially attractive to many customers, for he operated a small distillery on the premises. In addition to beer, he offered a variety of stronger drinks including rye whiskey, *kümmel*, cognac, rum, and gin.

A popular gathering spot for many years was Frederick Hermann's beer garden, located in the heart of the Sixth Ward on the east side of Hustisford Road (now North Fourth Street), just south of the bridge. Hermann had come from a wealthy patrician family in Baden where he worked in the family-owned tannery.

While Hermann's establishment was very well patronized, he had stiff competition from his neighbor just across the bridge, Ulrich Habhegger, whose complex was spread over several acres. In addition to the saloon itself there were wooden picnic tables and benches scattered about, and two outdoor bowling alleys. Habhegger even had his own private icehouse to make sure that his beer was properly cooled on hot summer days.

Cigar store "Indian" is really a Turk

This "Indian" which stood at the entrance to A. F. Miller's cigar store was not an Indian, but rather a "Turk" or "Moor." Miller bought the figure in the 1860s.

16

The ever-optimistic Baron von Bredow had a much smaller beer garden on the west side of the city on West Avenue (today West Main Street), just across the Chicago and Northwestern railroad tracks. His specialty was *Weißbeer*, a rather pale light beer (described by at least one local observer as "nauseous.")

Bernard Miller (called "Gentleman" Miller because of his extreme politeness and immaculate appearance) conducted the St. Julian Saloon for a time. It was considered an "elegant" establishment. Like a number of the other Forty-Eighter saloon operators, Miller followed this line of work briefly, then moved on. He went into the wholesale cigar business in the Fischer building for a while, and was a justice of the peace. Earlier he had been a co-owner of a flouring mill. After exhausting his opportunities in Watertown, Miller moved to Chicago where he became an Internal Revenue collector.

In 1854, the locally popular Boegel's Hall was taken over by M. D. Marx. The new proprietor was a defrocked Catholic priest who had married and had several children. Marx took pride in advertising that his establishment was German, with good German cooking and Milwaukee beer. Before coming to the city, he farmed for a time in nearby Richwood where he also operated a sawmill. Later he taught school in Beaver Dam and Milwaukee, and was the assistant register of deeds of Dodge County in Juneau.

Formerly a student of economics at the University of Hohenheim and later manager of a large estate in Germany, Louis Baehr emigrated to Watertown with his family. He farmed briefly, then he too became a saloonkeeper and restaurant owner. One of his few social activities was his membership in the *Turnverein*. Fortune did not smile on Baehr in America, and he lived out his years in a modest and unpretentious manner.

To many observers, the words "German" and "beer" are synonymous, or essentially so. Although Charles Ducasse's attempts at beermaking failed miserably, several of the Forty-Eighters felt they could earn some sort of living by making hard liquor, that is, distilled spirits.

The first money-making effort of Frederick Hermann after his arrival in Watertown was operating a small distillery. Franz Graefe and a brother together with Charles Grote and Henry Tigler had a distillery on the west side of the river, north of the Rough and Ready dam near the Plank Road bridge. Both Graefe and Tigler returned to Germany after a time, although the latter revisited Watertown in later years. In Germany, Tigler became the owner of a large brewery in Osnabrück.

Joseph Stoppenbach had formerly been one of two notaries public in Cologne, an office which then carried a far greater level of responsibility and authority than that same duty in the United States. He had suffered severe financial losses in Germany, apparently

Indian watering trough

This watering trough stood for many years at the intersection of West Main and Washington Streets. People drank from basins at the upper level, horses from those in the middle, and dogs at the bottom.

18

stemming from his involvement in the Revolution. He came to Watertown where his first business venture within the city was conducting a distillery. This enterprise was not successful and Stoppenbach turned to other efforts.

Sabbath Celebrations and the Fourth of July

Before the arrival of the Germans in the Watertown community, the Sabbath was piously observed since many of the first settlers were Yankees who adhered to the Puritan standards of New England. The contrasting attitude of the Germans was that Sunday was a day for rest, relaxation, and a good time. The restrictiveness of the Puritan Sabbath was "a thorn in the eye" of the Germans. These contradicting philosophies were put to the test in mid-1852.

That year the Germans decided to properly celebrate the Fourth of July, the Independence Day of their new homeland. Watertown had never seen a celebration such as this was to be, for the festive occasion fell on a Sunday. When the surprised Americans learned of the plans the Germans had made, they petitioned the governor to call out the militia to prevent a raucous celebration, but to no avail.

Early on the morning of the Fourth, before the Americans had stirred from their beds (one account reported the time to be four o'clock in the morning), a barrage of cannon salutes was fired in front of Hoeffner's brewery. Droves of German farmers from the area began to pour into the city to join their fellow countrymen in properly honoring America's independence. They came on foot and on horseback, and in wagons by the dozens. The assembly gathered near the William Tell House at the sharp bend in Oak Grove Street (today North Church Street and Park Street).

Under the leadership of Emil Rothe and Ernst Off, both of whom had been involved in the Revolution, a parade formed. With Rothe and Off on horseback at the head of the column, the Germans enthusiastically proceeded through the city streets to the Liberty Pole (which they called the *Freiheitsbaum* or freedom tree) on the west side of the river. There the *Liedertafel* sang several appropriate numbers, including one of the popular songs of the Revolution, "*Freiheit, die ich meine*" ("Freedom, which I mean").

19

The parade then reformed, and with its "cavalry" of mounted horsemen in the lead, marched through Watertown in an exuberant procession. As might be imagined, the Americans were quite unnerved by all of this unseemly activity. Threats were hurled at the processioners by some of the Yankees, and heated profanity was exchanged. But the Germans were not to be denied, and the event continued without incident.

"Exercises" were also conducted to honor the grand occasion; the orator for that event, which was conducted entirely in German, was Emil Rothe.

During the day, the celebrants gathered at Schulten's Garden and toasted America's freedom with beer and *Gemütlichkeit* (sociability). Despite the fact that many of the Americans had protested vehemently against the celebration and the desecration of the Sabbath, a number of them were seen enjoying the festivities at Schulten's. A torchlight parade that evening topped off the day's activities and brought to a close this landmark event of Watertown's early history.

The next day, Monday July 5, a second celebration was held, with the "exercises" being conducted in both German and English. The main speaker at that event, an American clergyman, went to some length to denounce one of the major events connected with the Revolution, the Frankfurt Assembly, "as a godless assemblage because when it was proposed to open the convention with prayer the members of the convention hissed." One might surmise that this opinion was not well received by the Forty-Eighter portion of the local population.

When 1854 arrived, the celebration of the Fourth began with a salute of thirty-two cannon shots. The following year, the English-language *Watertown Democrat* reported that it was glad to note that the Fourth of July would not pass unobserved "by the citizens of this place." It added that "the German portion of our population have taken hold of the matter in good earnest." After the 1855 celebration had taken place, the *Democrat* was enthusiastic in describing all that had transpired. It speculated that "thousands" must have marched in the procession "to the strains of spirit-stirring martial music."

A highlight of the "exercises" which took place that year at Marschauer's Gardens was the reading of the Declaration of Independence in German by Edward Pfenniger. Once the inspector of large estates in Germany, Pfenniger had a voice "that could be heard by an entire army corps." The *Democrat* commented that "it was something strange, yet particularly appropriate, in having [the Declaration] read in the presence of representatives of so many nations, on American soil in a Foreign tongue." It added, "the accomplished reader seemed to make the noble sentiments he repeated his own." Pfenniger served as a notary and a long-time justice of the peace in the city.

Gathering Spots

There were several favorite places where the Watertown Forty-Eighters would meet informally to discuss both lofty ideals and mundane problems. William Wiggenhorn's Buena Vista House was one such spot, primarily attracting bachelors. There they could shoot billiards, drink beer, smoke cigars, and "disputate." Local tradition has it that they would have rather formal debates from time to time in Greek or Latin.

Another establishment popular with the Forty-Eighters was Boegel's Hall, a combination saloon and hall. For a time it even included a casino. Some of its perceived elegance stemmed from the fact that the ceiling of the hall was painted light blue and a multitude of gold paper stars were affixed to it. Emil Rothe, Carl Schurz, Charles Ducasse and Theodore Bernhard were among its regular patrons. Otto Ruppius, who achieved wide recognition as one of the most widely-read German novelists of the nineteenth century, frequently stopped at Boegel's. He came to Watertown periodically from Milwaukee while working outside that city as a traveling wine salesman.

Jacob Karst, who operated *Zum Freischütz* for a time, later had an extremely popular saloon called *Der Stadtbrunnen* or "City Well." The Forty-Eighter element was attracted there also. Every morning customers would gather at Karst's to exchange small talk of the day. But more importantly, Karst's functioned as a miniature business forum. Business transactions of every kind were arranged or completed there, while property sites and buildings were bought and sold.

Newsmen and Newsmakers

Many of Watertown's Forty-Eighters had been well educated and had a strong interest in polemics and cultural affairs. One excellent outlet for those interests was newspaper work.

The German press of the city began in 1853 when David Blumenfeld and John Kopp established the *Watertown Anzeiger*. Their pitifully small quarters were in the rickety Fischer block, midstream above the Rock River. Their supply of type was so modest

Buena Vista House

The Buena Vista was considered to be one of the two "great German hotels of the West." From 1848 to 1863 it was operated by Forty-Eighter William Wiggenhorn. It was a popular gathering spot for local Forty-Eighters where they could shoot billiards, drink beer, and "disputate."

they were obliged to set one side of the page, print it, break down the type and return it to its case, then set the opposite side of the page and print it.

Blumenfeld and his partner had come to Watertown following strong encouragement from prominent German citizens of the city. Blumenfeld had received journeyman training in Germany and had previously followed his trade in several American cities including Milwaukee, where he was the foreman of Moritz Schoeffler's *Wisconsin Banner.*

Blumenfeld's political allegiance, and that of his paper, was always in loyal, unswerving support to the Democratic party. For over thirty years the publisher served as secretary of the local Democratic committee. Nevertheless he was a close friend of Carl Schurz, a prominent member of the opposing Republican party, particularly during the years that Schurz lived in Watertown. That friendship may have stemmed from their mutual love of the newspaper business. One afternoon in later years, Schurz and Blumen-

David Blumenfeld
Blumenfeld published Watertown's first German newspaper, the *Anzeiger*. It subsequently became the *Weltbürger*, and for many years had the largest circulation of any paper in the community. In the first decades of the 20th century, Blumenfeld's son, Ralph, was the editor of the London *Daily Express*, reported to be the largest newspaper in England, and one of the largest in the world.

feld sat in Blumenfeld's garden, enjoying cigars and reminiscing. Schurz commented to his friend that he would rather be a newspaperman and head of the *New York Herald* than president, king, or anything like it. By chance Blumenfeld's son Ralph was in the garden at the time and heard the remark. Ralph later claimed in his book *Home Town* that it was this single event that made him decide to become a newsman himself. He did, and was eminently successful in that career, ultimately becoming editor of the London *Daily Express*, which had the largest circulation in England and one of the largest in the world during the time he was its editor. David Blumenfeld remained in Watertown where he became a highly respected Wisconsin newspaperman who followed his craft for fifty-two years.

In October of 1857 a competing newspaper was founded locally, the *Weltbürger*. Its editor was Emil Rothe, a Forty-Eighter who had previously served as editor of the *Anzeiger*. During the period following Rothe's resignation from the *Anzeiger*, Schurz served as its editor for at least one week, possibly two. His political opinions were so different from those of the paper's owners that he was quickly dismissed from his editorial post, even though the English-language *Democrat* reported that he had purchased controlling interest in the *Anzeiger*. This appears to have been rumor rather than fact. Succeeding Schurz was another Forty-Eighter and former theologian, Joseph Engelmann.

In February of 1858 the *Weltbürger* and the *Anzeiger* joined forces under a new name, *Der Weltbürger und Anzeiger*, with Rothe as editor of the combined journal. On January 1, 1859, *Der Watertown Weltbürger* succeeded the latter publication with Blumenfeld as sole owner and Rothe as editor. This uncertain state of affairs came to a close when Rothe resigned as editor on June 20, 1862, and Blumenfeld took complete charge of the paper. He remained at the head of the operation until his death in 1905.

For many years an opinion prevailed in Watertown that the circulation of the *Weltbürger* had remained the highest of any newspaper in the city until it finally ceased publication in 1932. This was not the case. As the tide of German immigration began to subside in the late 1800s, subscriptions to the *Weltbürger* declined as well. The

American-born children of German parents began to assimilate, and did not maintain the language of *das Vaterland.* The *Weltbürger's* circulation steadily decreased after the turn of the century as the *Watertown Daily Times,* an English-language daily publication, became more widely read.

The German press had expanded in September of 1857 when Carl Schurz established the "radically Republican" *Volkszeitung.* Its editor was Hermann von Lindemann, who was assisted by Charles J. Palme. The journal, which was subsidized by the Republican party, survived through the 1860 presidential election, after which it ceased publication. The *Volkszeitung* was unique in that initially it was printed on one side of the page in German (written by Lindemann who dropped the "von" from his name), and the other in

Weltbürger office

The *Weltbürger* was the longest-lived German newspaper in Watertown, existing from 1857 to 1932. Like other papers of its day, it also did job-shop printing. Publisher David Blumenfeld who headed the paper for over fifty years stands at the right in the doorway.

English (written by Schurz). This format was eliminated after a time and the paper continued in German only.

Lindemann's local contemporaries recognized him as a writer of considerable ability. He had been the editor of the Dresden *Gazette* in Germany, but his heavy involvement in the Revolution led to his arrest and trial. He was condemned to death, but escaped and fled to the United States. He came to Watertown where he was considered a protégé of Schurz.

Lindemann's involvement in the American political process took him to Washington in 1860. He was a presidential elector for the ticket of Abraham Lincoln and served as the messenger to carry Wisconsin's official vote to the nation's capitol. He arrived in Washington one day too late to be able to cast his state's ballot.

Among the various positions Lindemann held after leaving Watertown late in 1861 was a role with the prestigious *Westliche Post* in Saint Louis, the same paper that Schurz was to join at a later date.

Palme, the one-time assistant editor of the *Volkszeitung*, went on to become the chief editor of the Milwaukee *Herold*. He subsequently headed a government paper factory in Massachusetts, an appointment he received through the influence of his friend Schurz.

Other Watertown Forty-Eighters who explored the newspaper field included Peter Bodien, briefly a contributor to the Milwaukee *Herold*, and Henry Colonius, who at the age of seventeen had been the youngest participant in the Revolution among Watertown's Forty-Eighters. Colonius served as editor of the *Staatszeitung* in Wheeling, Virginia (now West Virginia). He was strongly opposed to the secession of Virginia from the Union prior to the Civil War and voted twice against that proposition. When Virginia eventually did leave the Union, Colonius left the paper.

A distinguished writer who resided in Watertown for a time was Adolf Strodtmann, who spent the summer of 1857 in the city. The long-haired, blond, bespectacled Strodtmann was the admiring biographer of Gottfried Kinkel, one of the chief leaders of the Revolutionary forces. Strodtmann was also the translator of a number of American works into German, including *Uncle Tom's Cabin*. While in the city, he lived as a guest of both Schurz and Schurz's parents.

Noteworthy among Watertown's journalists was Emil Rothe. He was born September 23, 1826, in Guhrau on the Prussian-Polish border. As a young man he studied law at Breslau, Bonn, Jena, Heidelberg, and Berlin. He took part in various student assemblies at the time of the Revolution, and was the first president of the German Student's Association at Eisenach. He was succeeded in that position by Carl Schurz. For a time he reported to several newspapers about the proceedings of the assemblies in Frankfurt, including publications in France and Italy.

Following the failure of the Revolution, Rothe gradually made his way to the United States, arriving here in 1849. He was a strawberry farmer for a time in New Jersey, and in May of 1850 came to Watertown after having spent several months in Milwaukee. With Theodore Bernhard, Rothe established a cigarmaking business in the city. When Bernhard left that ill-fated undertaking to begin work as a notary, Rothe continued alone for only a short period. He sold the operation within the year to Ernst Grossmann and his brother, and established himself as a lawyer and notary.

Emil Rothe

Student at the universities of Breslau, Bonn, Jena, Heidelberg, Berlin; newsman, farmer, cigar manufacturer, lawyer, politician. Rothe grew strawberries in New Jersey and was one of Watertown's Latin farmers. He founded the Watertown *Weltbürger* which merged with Blumenfeld's *Anzeiger*. He was later an editor and lawyer in Cincinnati.

Rothe's interest in newspaper work brought him back to that field with the establishment of the *Weltbürger*. Following the merger of the *Weltbürger* with Blumenfeld's *Anzeiger*, Rothe became editor of the political portion of the paper while Blumenfeld served as publisher. Rothe's participation gradually dwindled until it was only a part-time occupation from which he ultimately resigned, for he was rapidly becoming involved in American politics. In his political activities, Rothe consistently and strongly supported the Democratic party. For twenty years, he was one of the most forceful and respected speakers for the candidates and causes of that party. It was reported locally that during every election, he received $500 for expenses as a Democrat campaigner.

In 1854 Rothe married Johanna Ducasse, daughter of fellow Forty-Eighter Squire Ducasse. He was first elected to public office in 1857 when he and Schurz became members of Watertown's city council. That same year he was also named justice of the peace for two wards.

In 1862 and again in 1864, Rothe was the candidate of the Democratic party for Secretary of State for Wisconsin. His defeats in those years were attributed to the votes of Union soldiers supporting Lincoln and his Republican party. In between these two unsuccessful bids for office, Rothe was elected to the State Assembly of Wisconsin in 1863.

Rothe was offered the position of chief editor of the Cincinnati *Volksfreund* in 1869. The job carried with it the enticing salary of $3000 yearly. "Take it, take it," was the advice of his friend Blumenfeld. After having lived in Watertown for seventeen years, Rothe moved to Ohio. Several years later, however, he reverted to the practice of law, for a time in partnership with one of his sons.

Taking into account his forceful writing, his political interests and his ambition, one might speculate that Rothe's move to Cincinnati was a reflection of his disappointment at failing to be elected Wisconsin's Secretary of State. Clearly he was aware of the success being realized by Schurz. There must have been a measure of bitterness at his failure to receive at least a portion of the acceptance that had come his way in Germany where he had been chosen to lead the student assembly at Eisenach before that post was taken over by Schurz. Emil Rothe died in Cincinnati on April 27, 1895, at the age of sixty-nine.

Rothe was a proud, enthusiastic German-born American. He contributed effectively in a variety of roles to his new homeland, and particularly to Watertown, his home for so many years. He was a marked asset to his adopted *Heimat* (homeland).

The Professors

When the hopeful young Forty-Eighters came to Watertown in the late 1840s and mid-1850s, their immediate needs were to earn a living by whatever means, and to build or acquire a place to live. A few were able to take advantage of the training they had received in Germany. Several were teachers, while some were termed "professors," a rather loosely applied definition.

Emil C. Gaebler taught music and languages in Connecticut for seven years before coming to Wisconsin; he settled in Watertown in 1858. He gave private music lessons in a studio adjacent to his organ-building shop on North Fourth Street. On occasion Gaebler had his students perform on their instruments in the studio while he worked at some task in his shop. Though he was often out of sight, a student who struck a wrong note would promptly hear a shout from his teacher, "*Falsch* (wrong)."

Frederick Hoeper was one of the many talented émigrés who came to Watertown. Prior to coming to the United States, he had been the private secretary and business manager of a wealthy Dutch count. After he left Europe, Hoeper briefly looked for gold in the California gold fields. He came to Watertown in 1854, farmed for a short time, and conducted one of the local singing societies. He gave intermittent piano and dancing instruction, an effort which brought only modest success. Nevertheless, Hoeper appeared to his contemporaries to be totally content while thoughtfully smoking his pipe. In later years, when prospective students no longer sought him out as a teacher, he worked for a time as a bookkeeper for brewer Joseph Bursinger, and later did "handwork" at Hartig and Manz's brewery.

One misfit among the Forty-Eighter element was Georg Hugo Licht who came from a very wealthy family in Fraustadt, Posen. His father had been a landowner of considerable wealth. Licht studied law at both Breslau and Berlin.

Unfortunately, Licht managed to dissipate the rather sizable fortune that came his way through an extravagant and wild lifestyle. He came to America in 1849 and made his living in the east as an artist, and as a piano and language teacher. In 1867 he came to live in Watertown with his nephew, Emil Rothe.

For a time, Licht earned a modest income as an artist. In later years, he tended one of the newfangled beer-bottling machines in Bursinger's brewery. Yet his bitter sarcasm, his continuing discontent with his lot, made Licht an unhappy and angry old man who withdrew into stubborn silence. His strange behavior caused the community to regard him as "eccentric." When he died in 1885, it was said that the cause of his death was starvation, for he had been too proud, or perhaps too stubborn, to ask for help.

The gods were equally unkind to Louis W. Ranis. He came from a well-to-do family, and for a time was an archaeologist. He arrived in Watertown in 1848, and was one of the communities' short-duration Latin farmers.

Frederick Hoeper

In Europe Hoeper had been the private secretary and business manager of a Dutch count. After coming to America, he looked for gold in California, and ultimately settled in Watertown where he gave piano and dancing lessons.

Ranis taught briefly as a professor of Latin at the local Northwestern College. He had attended three universities and was considered "overeducated" among his fellow townsmen, as well as "eccentric." On occasion he was the "leader" or "lay pastor" of the local *Freie Gemeinde*, the Free Congregation. After living in Watertown for forty years, Ranis moved to La Crosse, Wisconsin where he died in the county poorhouse.

A more successful educator was Theodore Bernhard. He was instrumental in bringing the public school system of Watertown to a position of prominence in the state. Bernhard was born in Berlin in 1820. He attended the university there, studying philology and philosophy. Following graduation, he served as a private tutor for some of the families of the nobility who lived in the city. He had been promised a professorship at the university which made him suspect during the Revolution. He had to flee during the period of reaction, and arrived in Watertown in 1849.

Bernhard's ill-fated venture into cigarmaking with Emil Rothe did not last long. He was appointed a notary public and shortly after that, a justice of the peace. His reputation for integrity and impartiality was soon evident, and he was elected to a seat in the State Assembly in 1854. The following year he served as Watertown's city clerk.

In 1859 Bernhard returned to teaching, his first love. He opened a private school with a partner in the former home of Squire Ducasse at the southwest corner of North Fifth and Jones Streets. One unidentified early-day Watertown teacher had insisted it was enough for students to learn only the basics of "readin', 'ritin', and 'rithmetic," and that grammar was "Yankee humbuggery." This was an unacceptable philosophy to Bernhard. His students were exposed to a wide range of subjects including mathematics (which encompassed trigonometry), history, reading, spelling, writing, languages, philosophy, chemistry, astronomy, and physics.

Almost all of Bernhard's instruction was without the use of textbooks; only German reading and literature were taught with them. Bernhard also insisted on good penmanship. To accomplish that end, from time to time he would dictate a series of exercises which the students would write in blank notebooks. Later he would correct each individually, with marginal notes telling the student how to improve his work.

One of the earliest assignments for Bernhard's pupils was learning the German alphabet. Bernhard prepared a number of 4" x 4" cards, each with one letter on it. He would hold up a letter before the students, then single out one scholar to name it, after which the entire class would repeat it in unison. With this method, the entire class quickly learned the whole alphabet. The same method was employed to teach his students entire words. This approach began with short, monosyllabic words, then longer words were added as the scholars progressed in their learning skills. When students were in the process of learning new words under this method, the pupil picked to pronounce the word would recite it rapidly, twice in succession. It would then be repeated by the entire class. If a word had two or more syllables, the last was doubled. The state of the Union in which the students lived was thus pronounced, "Wis-con-sin-sin, Wisconsin." Progress using this technique was reported to be "both rapid and remarkable."

Theodore Bernhard
Bernhard had studied at the University of Berlin, then became involved in the Revolution. He eventually came to Watertown where he earned wide recognition as the "father" of the local public school system. He was elected a member of the Wisconsin State Assembly in 1854.

While Latin was one of the subjects in his curriculum, Bernhard violently objected to the so-called "Oxford" form of Latin. "It is only a fool," he would shout, "who would call Pahter Payter." Bernhard's students obviously learned to pronounce the word as "Pahter."

Scientific subjects were always of great interest to Bernhard and he stayed abreast of the latest developments in science. His demonstrations in physics always delighted his students; so one of his punishments for an errant pupil was to deny him the privilege of watching such an experiment.

On occasion when a student was unruly, Bernhard would send him to a corner of the room, sometimes with his face to the wall. This punishment, taking place in front of the entire class, usually had a salutary effect; offenses were seldom repeated.

In certain cases, the disobedient student was brought to the front of the room and was made to stand there, holding the bent handle of Bernhard's walking stick close to — but not touching — his nose. This method also seemed to produce results. If events especially vexed the heavily bearded Bernhard, he would lash out verbally by deriding the student, *"Du Esel, du*! (you jackass, you!)."

Bernhard instructed the older students in his school in classrooms on the second floor, while his associate occupied the first floor and taught the younger pupils. Bernhard's scholars were seated in two separate classrooms where he paced back and forth between the rooms, instructing both groups simultaneously and keeping them both busy. Periodically he would stop and inhale a proper amount of snuff which he had taken from the oval wooden snuffbox that was his inseparable companion.

Over a period of years, instruction that was originally given in German switched to English. While Bernhard had had university training as a philologist, his skills in the latter language often produced comical results. His broken English brought an occasional state of hilarity to his American students who mimicked his mistakes.

By all accounts Bernhard was a strict and often hard taskmaster. While his students admired him, they generally avoided calling him by the properly respectful titles *"Herr Professor"* or "Mister." He was most frequently called "Theodore" by his charges in every age group; it was almost as though he was considered a contemporary by his students. Yet Bernhard rarely called pupils by their first names; the existing custom of using the student's last name as a form of address prevailed.

One feature of Bernhard's education policies was that classes were not held on Wednesday afternoon, but they were in session on Saturday morning. Quite obviously the latter were not popular, but in warmer weather there frequently were picnics in nearby groves on the afternoons that classes were not held. Prizes were awarded for various contests. The prime mover of all of these events, as one might expect, was Bernhard himself.

It is unclear when Bernhard became the superintendent of the Watertown School system. It was probably about 1875, yet he

Bernhard and his teachers
Theodore Bernhard is shown here surrounded by his teaching staff, probably from the public schools.

appears to have been the "unofficial" head of all the schools some time earlier.

One of the changes Bernhard implemented was the establishment of a "graded" school system. Pupils were promoted to a higher level of learning only after satisfactorily completing the courses at a given earlier level. The local press asserted that the Watertown school board was consistently governed by Bernhard's suggestions, and that his "great diligence and untiring devotion" brought the once-troubled local school system to a level of perfection matched by few other Wisconsin public schools.

Theodore Bernhard was afflicted by ill health much of his life; his primary ailment was chronic tuberculosis. During his last few years, his family and friends frequently begged him to retire. He refused, and died in 1879 at the age of fifty-nine in the city that had become his home.

Bernhard's private school

For several years, Bernhard operated a private school in the former home of Forty-Eighter Charles Ducasse. He taught on the upper floor while an assistant conducted classes on the lower level.

While Margarethe Schurz was not a part of the Forty-Eighter movement, it is appropriate to note that she established the first kindergarten in the United States in Watertown in November or December of 1856. This event occurred during the period that the Schurz family lived in the city. The school was located at the southwest corner of North Second and Jones Streets. Latter-day recognition of the importance of this contribution by the wife of the renowned Carl Schurz came in 1958 when a newly-created elementary school on the south side of Watertown was named "Schurz School" in her honor.

Margarethe Schurz and America's first kindergarten
Margarethe Schurz, wife of the great German-American Carl Schurz, founded the first kindergarten in the United States in Watertown in 1856. Pupils were instructed in German. These mannequins appear in the reconstructed original building which is now located on the grounds of the Watertown Historical Society.

Legal Practice

To become a practicing lawyer was a difficult goal to achieve for any Forty-Eighter of Watertown. For those who had been trained in law back in Germany, there was the language barrier. In addition, there were the laws of a new nation, and of a state within that nation to be learned, together with a practical knowledge of how those laws applied. This was a considerable body of information to be absorbed.

It was nevertheless easier in those days to become a practicing lawyer in Jefferson County (in which most of Watertown is situated) than it is today. When a candidate felt he was ready, a practicing Watertown lawyer would present an application to the county judge on behalf of the aspirant who accompanied him. The judge would review the document, then smile pleasantly and sign the required forms. All would then shake hands and adjourn to the nearest available saloon to properly celebrate the momentous occasion.

While ten of the Watertown Forty-Eighters had acquired legal training either in Germany or in America, they were not always able to follow a legal career in the United States. One of the new arrivals who fit this mold was Peter Bodien. Bodien came from Schleswig and had practiced law on the island of Föhr back home. Forced to flee because of his involvement in the Revolution in Schleswig-Holstein, he came first to Milwaukee in 1851. There he worked for a time as a reporter for the Milwaukee *Herold*. In 1855 Bodien moved to Watertown where he operated a grocery store on Third Street until his death in 1876. One of his daughters married Forty-Eighter Henry Steger, while another married a son of Forty-Eighter Daniel Kusel.

Joseph Stoppenbach, born near Cologne in 1800, entered the University of Bonn at the age of seventeen where he studied law. After graduation he opened a practice and soon thereafter was named a notary in Cologne, one of two in the entire city. A notary was an appointee, a lawyer who had the authority to prepare wills and probate them. He could also make conveyances of real estate.

37

Severe financial losses stemming from his involvement in the Revolution brought Stoppenbach to the United States in 1848. Initially he settled on a farm in the Richwood area, northwest of Watertown. When that endeavor did not succeed, he came to Watertown where he opened a distillery. When his son Charles was elected Register of Deeds for Jefferson County in 1854, Stoppenbach took the assistant's position under him and moved south to the nearby county seat, Jefferson. He remained in that city the rest of his life where he began a title and abstract business. He served as Register of Deeds himself from 1863 through 1865. Despite his extensive legal training in Germany, Stoppenbach did not practice in Watertown. Several years after settling in Jefferson, however, he reestablished himself as an attorney with a partner in a firm known as Clothier and Stoppenbach.

The most unusual of Watertown's Forty-Eighter residents who had legal training was John L. Kube. He had studied jurisprudence first in Berlin for three years, then in Posen for nine months. Later he expanded his qualifications in the courts of Birnbaum for over three years. From there he moved on to Frankfurt an der Oder, thence to Königsberg where he served as an Associate Judge.

Kube came to the United States in 1854, and after residing in New York state and in several Wisconsin cities, moved to Watertown in 1858. Although he was both a deputy sheriff and a justice of the peace, Kube could not avoid continuing brushes with the law; he seemed to have a remarkable ability to get into trouble.

In mid-1875, Kube was living in a house in the Fifth Ward on the city's northwest side. The home was owned by a Saint Louis woman, once a local resident. Shortly before the time in question, a fire had mysteriously broken out in the house causing extensive damage. The owner's husband, aided by neighbors, successfully extinguished the blaze. The episode was generally regarded as arson by Kube's neighbors, and Kube himself was considered the suspect.

One day soon afterward, the sixty-four year old mother of the owner went to the Kube residence with hammer and nails to board over windows that had been broken or removed during the fire. Kube objected to her actions, picked up a double-barrelled shotgun and pointed it at her. The woman attempted to resist, and in the ensuing struggle, the gun went off close to her head.

Still holding her hammer firmly, the old lady whacked Kube on his head. The blow opened a gaping wound, and left Kube's head soaked with blood. Another blow badly bashed his nose. Amid loud cursing and screaming, Kube finally broke away, leaving the woman badly battered. A warrant was later served on the old lady as she lay in her bed, while one was served on Kube as well; the latter called for his arrest for "intent to kill."

In 1876, Kube was twice arrested, once for obtaining money fraudulently, once on a felony count. Kube's last known major misdeed occurred in 1882 when he was convicted in Madison for forgery and sentenced to seven years imprisonment in the state prison. While Kube had been found guilty of many offenses over the years, he had an uncanny ability to avoid real punishment. Detailed searches of many sources fail to disclose even one case where he was either fined, or reprimanded, or penalized in any way, including serving the seven year sentence mentioned above.

The best known of the Watertown Forty-Eighter lawyers was Carl Schurz. He was admitted to the Wisconsin bar in 1858 while a resident of Watertown and formed a partnership in Milwaukee the following year with Halbert B. Paine under the name of Schurz and Paine. Schurz chose his partner well. Paine was a well-qualified lawyer who later served with distinction as a colonel in the Civil War, where he lost a leg. He subsequently was elected to the Congress of the United States and was to remain Schurz's lifelong friend. The rapid ascension of Schurz in the Wisconsin and national political arenas left only limited time to practice law. The bulk of the legal services performed by the firm of Schurz and Paine was carried on by Paine.

The most active of the Forty-Eighters in terms of the legal profession were Henry Colonius and Charles Grote. Colonius first came to the United States in March 1849, and was a cigar manufacturer in New York City for eight years. This was followed briefly by a teaching position, then by his newsman's career as editor of the Wheeling (Virginia) *Staatszeitung*.

At the outbreak of the Civil War, Colonius returned to Germany for a short time to attend to family business, then in 1862 came back to America and settled in the Watertown area. After farming for several years in nearby Richwood, he moved into the city and established a produce and wool commission business with his brother, Carl. That endeavor was followed by a brief return to cigarmaking.

Following several years' involvement in township and county-level elective posts, Colonius ran for the position of county judge of Jefferson County in 1877. He was chosen by the voters and remained in that office until his death nineteen years later. Colonius was considered a man of fine cultural tastes. He wrote both poetry and prose for the *Weltbürger* under the pseudonym "S."

Charles Grote operated a distillery with others during the years he lived in Watertown. In 1849 he had come directly to the city as a twenty-two year old, after having received a university education in Germany. His business ventures in Watertown were unfruitful, and in 1857 he moved to Germantown (Juneau County), Wisconsin.

Henry Colonius
At the age of seventeen, Colonius took an active role in the Revolution. He fled to the United States, worked as a newsman, then went back to Germany briefly. He returned to America in 1865, farmed for a time, and eventually became a judge of Jefferson County.

There he opened a grocery store, and after serving in several lesser county government offices, ran for county judge in 1869. He was elected, and held that office for over thirty years.

There is no evidence that either Judge Colonius or Judge Grote had any formal legal training, or had practiced law prior to being elected judge. Both, brimming with self-confidence and supported by enthusiastic friends and neighbors, simply ran for office, were elected, and instantly became judges.

Henry Mulberger was perhaps the most remarkable of Watertown's Forty-Eighters who ventured to the city and stayed. He came from Speyer in Rhenish Bavaria where his father was mayor of the city in 1848. Members of his distinguished family had served earlier in that same capacity in Speyer at intervals for 350 years.

North side of Main Street, west of North Second Street (@1866)
The flour and feed store at the right was probably that of John W. Cole. A portion of the large building to the left housed Colonius Brothers who were commission merchants; Forty-Eighter Henry Colonius was one of its partners. The center building cannot be identified.

Mulberger was born in 1824, and after schooling in the gymnasium and academy in Darmstadt, joined his father in their family-owned woolen goods manufacturing business. He came to Watertown in 1848 after brief stays in New York City and Ohio. He arrived with $10, 000 in gold, a sum that by present-day standards would have a value of approximately a quarter million dollars.

Mulberger's first business venture in Watertown was a grocery store. On one occasion, before the Watertown Plank Road existed, he traveled to Milwaukee to buy a supply of whiskey. The way was muddy and almost impassable. On the return trip, he bogged down on three occasions, and as a result, had to be pulled out of his predicament by teams of oxen. In Brookfield, Mulberger unloaded three barrels of his cargo to lighten the weight of his wagon. His miserable journey took three days, and when he finally did arrive in Watertown, only one barrel of whiskey remained.

Mulberger abandoned the grocery trade in 1852 to study law, and after four years was admitted to the Wisconsin bar. Initially he was a partner in the local firm of Enos and Hall, but in 1858 chose to go into private practice. Soon afterward, however, he formed a partnership with Harlow S. Orton, formerly chief justice of the Wisconsin Supreme Court. That association was dissolved in 1860. He subsequently established a new partnership with Major Charles H. Gardner which continued for many years. Gardner had the distinction of being the only Watertown volunteer to fight for the South during the Civil War; there he rode with the Confederate cavalry under General Kirby Smith.

Mulberger was considered to be one of the finest "office" lawyers in the state and rarely appeared in court. His opinion in complex legal issues was regularly sought by fellow attorneys; his advice was usually correct.

All of these legal ventures were being carried on while Mulberger's restless and ambitious nature took him into a variety of other business undertakings. His legal background undoubtedly served him well in these efforts.

In 1858 Mulberger was one of the original founders of the Jefferson County Bank, which was later known as the Wisconsin National Bank. He served long as a vice president and director of that institution. He also found time somehow to become the president of the Globe Milling Company. Additionally, he had extensive property holdings in Watertown and vicinity, as well as in North Dakota and Michigan. And in 1861, he founded a tannery.

Mulberger was a pioneer in the field of insurance, particularly fire insurance, and was considered its "pathfinder" within Watertown. He was known to pay insurance premiums out of his own pocket on many occasions when a financially-troubled policy holder was unable to scrape together the money himself. He was the local agent for one insurance firm for thirty-three years and was reported to be the "oldest" (possibly meaning "longest tenured") insurance agent in the entire country when he resigned.

Mulberger had spent his early years in Speyer, an area where winemaking was a longstanding tradition. So it was quite natural that this enterprising German created a three acre vineyard within the city. He grew Catawba, Isabella, and Delaware grapes primarily after having experimented with other types. The wine he ultimately produced was known as "Rock River Wine" and was popular locally.

Mulberger's inexhaustible energy reached into the area of public service also. In 1853-54, he was a local justice of the peace; in the latter year he served as clerk of the municipal court as well as city clerk. He held the position of city attorney from 1856 through 1858. In 1865 he was the alderman from his ward, and from 1877 through 1879 he sat on the county board.

Mulberger's highest civic honor came in the spring of 1867 when his fellow citizens chose him as mayor of Watertown. With that selection, the family tradition begun hundreds of years earlier in Speyer had continued. It was prolonged even further when each of his sons, Henry, Charles, and Arthur, was elected mayor of the city as well. Mulberger was the only Forty-Eighter to fill the mayor's post of the community.

When he first arrived in the country, Mulberger was a Whig, or conservative Liberal. But after a short time, he switched his allegiance to the Democratic party. He followed most of its beliefs, but was not blindly loyal to it. Notwithstanding these political leanings, Mulberger was a close friend of Republican Carl Schurz. While the two differed on political issues, the bonds of friendship were strong. Moreover, Schurz admired his friend's legal skills to such an extent that Mulberger served as Schurz's lawyer on occasion.

Unlike most of his local fellow Forty-Eighters, Mulberger was able to return to Germany for one visit, in 1857. It was necessitated by events relating to the settlement of his father's estate. Within a single month after returning to the "old country," he wrote to friends back in Watertown from his former home town of Speyer telling them, "I [quickly] became heartily sick of [Germany] — a strange feeling." He described his old homeland as "this dull old place." Henry Mulberger had become an American. The redeeming feature of the trip was meeting Mathilde Wolf, daughter of a highly-placed government official in Hesse. He was so enchanted that he married her there before returning home to America.

Henry Mulberger died in Watertown on January 19, 1896 of stomach cancer at the age of seventy-two. His many business undertakings and his boundless enthusiasm helped make his home

Dr. Clemens Eger
Eger was a close friend of Carl Schurz whom he known in Germany, and of Emil Rothe. He was educated at the universities of Dresden and Leipzig, and was highly regarded as a physician.

in the United States a city of stature within his own lifetime. He was an outstanding Watertownian.

The Medical Practitioners

Three physicians were among the new Forty-Eighters who arrived in Watertown. Each was well received by the local populace. The most prominent of these emigrants was Dr. Clemens T. Eger. He had attended the universities in Leipzig and Dresden, married, and came to Watertown with his wife and infant son in 1856. Eger was a close friend of Carl Schurz, whom he had known in Germany. That friendship continued in Watertown where Eger also numbered Emil Rothe and David Blumenfeld among his close companions.

The local newspapers characterized him as "highly esteemed," and "one of nature's noblemen," with a "wonderfully clear memory." Despite these high-sounding accolades, Eger was some-

Dr. Carl R. Feld
First a pharmacist, later a physician, Feld had studied in both Berlin and Würzburg. He was persuaded to come to Watertown by another local Forty-Eighter, Charles Jacobi. His son, Carl, served in the Wisconsin State Assembly.

thing of a non-conformist. He avoided the generally accepted dress code of his peers, and looked instead, as one observer reported, "like a plumber's helper."

The career of Dr. Carl R. Feld was more varied than that of many of the Forty-Eighters in Watertown. He was born in Kreuznach, the son of a pharmacist. He also studied pharmacy, then came to America in the mid-1840s and worked at that profession. He returned to Germany in 1848 and studied medicine at the universities of Würzburg and Berlin. He returned to the United States after completing his schooling and settled briefly in New York and Milwaukee, then came to Watertown in 1857 at the urging of another Watertown Forty-Eighter, Charles Jacobi.

Every account of Feld describes him as a man of honor, conscientious, trustworthy, without enemies. His son, Carl R. Feld, Jr.,who also became a doctor, served as a member of the Wisconsin State Assembly.

Dr. Christian Fischer came from Förste in Hanover. He studied at the University of Göttingen, and arrived in Watertown in 1848. He left the city briefly to practice in nearby Hustisford, then returned to Watertown in 1849 to take over the practice of Dr. Louis Meyer, who had moved to California. He enjoyed an excellent reputation among his fellow practitioners, particularly as a surgeon, and a setter of broken bones.

Public Service

The majority of the Forty-Eighters who came to Watertown had no apparent intention of returning to Germany. They settled with the expectation of making the community their home in a new homeland. One of the best measures of their commitment to their new country is in their frequent public service. They were office holders at the city, township, county, state, and national levels.

The first of the local Forty-Eighters elected to office was Frederick Hermann. His fellow townsmen picked him as an alderman in the spring of 1853. Henry Mulberger and Ernst Off were chosen in 1854 as city clerk and city marshal respectively. The highest level of local dominance by the Forty-Eighters came in 1857. Schurz,

Rothe, and Hermann were aldermen; Mulberger was the city attorney; and Ducasse the city surveyor. The city marshal continued to be Off; Rothe was justice of the peace for two wards; Schurz the supervisor for two wards; and Edward Pfenniger served as a constable.

The Forty-Eighter with the greatest involvement in Watertown's government was Henry Bieber. Bieber was an idealist who held many beliefs that he seemingly was unable to carry out during the many years he lived in the city. He was attending his last semester at the University of Erlangen studying theology and philology when he became very committed to the Revolution. His participation caused him to be thrown in prison for a year, and his theological career came to an abrupt halt. After release from his fortress cell, Bieber married and lived in the Zweibrücken area with his wife and father-in-law. For a time he leased both a mill and an inn in the vicinity.

Bieber was something of a recluse, especially in his later years. He could almost always be found at his home when he was not

Frederick Hermann
Hermann came from a wealthy family in Baden. He had many businesses in Watertown, including a saloon, summer garden, lime kiln, tannery. He also served as the city treasurer and as a county supervisor.

fulfilling his municipal duties. The only hobby he was known to have was writing poetry, apparently only in German. He and his wife, however, were active in the local *Turnverein*. Those doings were related to the theatrical enterprises of the club. He often served as the prompter in stage shows presented by the Turners.

At the time of his death, the four local papers were unanimous in lauding his wide-ranging contributions to Watertown in his city clerk's role. But the *Weltbürger* caught the old revolutionary spirit of Henry Bieber in relating that "the flame of passion burned in his breast for the idealistic good of mankind, for truth, light [enlighten-ment], freedom, justice, and humanity."

One measure of the confidence their fellow citizens had for several of these Forty-Eighters was electing them to major public office beyond the local level. This was during a period in American history when it was an honor to be chosen to serve, not an obliga-tion or curse (as some persons feel about elective office today).

Thus it was a singular accolade that four of the Watertown Forty-Eighters were elected to the State Assembly of Wisconsin. Theodore Bernhard was the first to be recognized. He went to Madison in 1854, and was soon known as a strong opponent of anti-liquor legislation. When one such piece of legislation was proposed that year, Bernhard spoke out strongly against it before the Assembly.

Bernhard was followed to the Assembly in 1860 by Hermann H. Winter, a farmer who lived south of the city. Winter had attended the University of Göttingen where he studied theology. He was a classmate of Otto von Bismarck and "spoke perfect Greek, Latin, English." He is believed to have been an ordained minister, and on occasion was referred to as "Reverend."

In 1863, the year between his two unsuccessful attempts at the office of Secretary of State for Wisconsin, Emil Rothe became a State Assembly member. The fourth Watertownian to be picked for membership in the distinguished Assembly was Franz G. L. Struve. He also was a farmer who lived south of the city. Struve served as register of deeds for Jefferson County for two terms in the early 1860s. In 1868 he was voted into the Assembly. Little is known about Struve, but it is apparent that he was a highly regarded new

American. He was appointed to serve as Consul General of the United States in Quebec, Canada, and died there in that post, the night before his scheduled departure for Leghorn, Italy where he was being reassigned as Consul.

It was at the national level that Carl Schurz received his greatest recognition in the United States. He served as the country's Minister to Spain (1861), as United States senator (from Missouri, 1869 - 1875), and as Secretary of the Interior in the cabinet of President Rutherford B. Hayes (1877 - 81).

There is no evidence to suggest that the local Forty-Eighters ever controlled Watertown's governmental bodies, or that they even attempted to do so. They appear to have been satisfied with being part of the political process. Neither is there any evidence that they tried to take charge of any social organization within the city.

The pride that Watertown's Forty-Eighters had in their new homeland is well demonstrated in one small, yet significant, way. When the *Watertown Democrat* published a list of the registered voters of the city in 1868, twenty years after the Revolution that had brought them to Wisconsin, the names of twenty-eight of the Forty-Eighters appeared. At least nineteen of their group had died or moved elsewhere, while the voting status or residence of the remaining fourteen could not be determined with certainty. Thus, among the forty-seven of the Forty-Eighter group still in Watertown or its immediate vicinity, more than three out of four had achieved voting status.

Religious Affiliations

Throughout its entire history, Watertown has been home to a number of churches, perhaps to a greater extent than many of its neighboring communities. Most of the major religious denominations found in the United States have been represented with local parishes. The most dominant of the groups has been the Lutheran church, represented by several synodal affiliations.

While Forty-Eighters as a group tended to be non-religious or even anti-religious, religion was a factor in the lives of several in Watertown. The strongest religious affiliation was with a local *Freie*

Gemeinde, a "Free Congregation." The *Gemeinde* of Watertown was established in 1848 as the German Evangelical Church. Its first meeting place was the hall of the Buena Vista House. Among its later names were the Free Evangelical Protestant Church and the Free Protestant Church (to which was sometimes added "Germ." indicating "German.") The *Gemeinde* eventually changed its name in 1909 and became St. Luke's Lutheran Church.

Basic to the belief of the thirty or so *Gemeinden* in Wisconsin was preserving the independence of both the individual and the congregation. Members were considered to be "separatists" or "dissenters," frequently having broken off their affiliation with established religious authority; this separation was sometimes prompted by a desire to adhere to no existing theology. Hence the word "Free" as part of their formal name. Each local organization represented the highest level of accepted authority; there were no specific beliefs required of members. A written statement of the principles of a congregation was the credo by which its members united — and there were often many such declarations. Typical of these beliefs

Freie Gemeinde
The *Freie Gemeinde* in Watertown was located on North Fourth street. It was a "free" congregation in its early years, not following the beliefs of any of the established religions. It eventually became St. Luke's Lutheran Church.

were tenets such as these: reason replaced revelation; knowledge substituted for faith; for trust in God, use self-reliance; for heaven in another world, heaven in this world; for the pastor or preacher, the speaker (who led the services).

It was not until 1850 that a pastor (or speaker) of the Watertown *Gemeinde* was installed. Among its temporary "leaders" were Forty-Eighters Hermann Winter and Louis W. Ranis. Frederick Brandt, another Forty-Eighter and local merchant, was a long-time trustee; his wife headed the ladies' *Verein* (society) for many years. Other Forty-Eighters with ties to the *Gemeinde* were Theodore Bernhard, Dr. Christian Fischer, Frederick Hermann, Frederick Hoeper, Charles Jacobi, Jacob Karst, Charles Paraski.

Occasionally identified with the *Gemeinde* movement were the Sons of Hermann. They came into being within the membership of the Masonic Order. The primary purposes of this organization were the prevention of poverty and suffering, giving aid to the sick, and assisting family survivors when a member died. It was not unlike many of the latter-day fraternal insurance and mutual aid societies. Gutenberg Lodge No. 13 of the Sons of Hermann was organized in Watertown on April 17, 1871. Among the Forty-Eighters who were members were David Blumenfeld, Emil C. Gaebler, Otto Linde, Theodore Bernhard, and Phillip Schmidt.

The more established religions played a role in the lives of several Watertown Forty-Eighters. Daniel Kusel, Sr., a hardware merchant, helped to organize the Lutheran Church in the city. The first parish was St. John's, which was created in 1852. Kusel was a member of another early Lutheran parish in the city, St. Mark's, which was founded in 1854. He took an active role in the founding of the local *Lutherisches College,* a Lutheran seminary that ultimately became known as Northwestern College.

Joseph Salick, a watchmaker, was one of the founders of the German Catholic church, St. Henry's. He was among the handful of Germans who came to Watertown following the Revolution who had been "on the other side." Another was Rev. Max de Beck, a strong and stately-looking priest (considered more military than religious in his bearing), who became the pastor of St. Henry's. He led that parish from early 1862 until late 1864. De Beck was

Hungarian-born and came from a distinguished family. He served for a time as a military chaplain, and when the fortress Komorn was besieged in 1848 by Louis Kossuth and his followers, was among its defenders.

One of the attacking Austrians during this same engagement at Komorn was Ignatz Jahna. He later served in the Austrian army in Italy with the military police and came to America in 1867 with his wife and children. He settled northwest of Watertown in near Richwood where he farmed for the remainder of his life. Jahna became a member of St. Henry's parish after coming to the area.

Catholicism was strong in the family of Carl Schurz, though he himself rejected that religion as a youth. His first cousin, Johann Christian Schurz, came to Watertown as a young man and worked as a clerk in the local post office for several years. After leaving Watertown and wandering to other parts of the United States, Schurz went to Milwaukee where he studied theology and was ordained a priest. Father Schurz was the first resident pastor of Wichita, Kansas and served for many years in both Kansas and Illinois.

The anti-religious (or non-religious) attitudes so frequently ascribed to the Forty-Eighters was also evident in Watertown. Henry Bieber, the long-time city clerk, had studied theology but did not follow any religion after his involvement in the Revolution. Joseph Engelmann, the one-time newspaperman, had been a student of theology and may have been an ordained clergyman; he, too, apparently dropped the practice of formal religion. Organ manufacturer Emil C. Gaebler similarly had examined theology but definitely did not pursue that calling. M. D. Marx, a one-time Catholic priest who later became a saloonkeeper, clearly departed from the religious life.

Unique among the religious pursuits of the Watertown Forty-Eighters was the choice of Henry Mulberger. It is unknown whether he followed any established faith while still in Europe, but in Watertown he became a member of St. Paul's Episcopal Church. One can only speculate as to why Mulberger made this choice. His home back in Germany was in the cathedral city of Speyer, located in a heavily Catholic area. He may have followed Catholicism since it would have been the "state" or "official" church there at the time. A number of Watertown's early settlers had come from New England where the Episcopal church was a dominant entity. Moreover, six of the first twelve presidents of the United States had adhered to that faith. Thus when Mulberger came to Watertown, his decision to join the Episcopal church may have been prompted by his perception that it was the closest equivalent to a "state" church in America.

Artisans and Craftsmen, by Training or Necessity

The popular conception of the Forty-Eighters is that virtually all were young, idealistic, militant university students who fought tyranny and oppression, and who struggled to achieve freedom and rights. While that belief has some validity, Professor Theodore S. Hamerow has very properly observed "that the truth is that for every Carl Schurz among the [German] immigrants there were hundreds who wanted nothing more than a secure livelihood." Artisans and craftsmen were among this group and a number came to Watertown.

Johann Strauss moved to the United States with his new bride in 1852. After a three-year stay in New York, he relocated in Watertown. The couple settled on a farm three miles south of the city and lived there for two years. Strauss then disposed of the farm and established himself as a master shoemaker in Watertown in 1857. Within a short time he had a wide following because of his skill and his likable personality. Strauss was the only Forty-Eighter who belonged to the Moravian church; his farm had been located in the center of a settlement of fellow church members who attended the Ebenezer Moravian Church in the farmland south of the city.

West of Watertown in nearby Waterloo, L. H. Trayser set up shop as a cabinetmaker. After participating in the Revolution in 1848 and 1849, he came to America in 1852. He spent several years in Philadelphia and Baltimore, then moved to the Midwest. In the early 1860s he opened a furniture business in Waterloo, which he continued until his death in 1898 at the age of seventy-two.

Henry Peters began his training as a tailor at the age of fifteen. While traveling as a journeyman under the fading guild system, he lived in several major cities in Germany. He then settled in Berlin where he resided for five years. After taking an active part in the Revolution, he came to America in 1851 and landed in New York. As did many of the immigrants who arrived with little or no money, Peters remained in New York and other eastern cities for four years. He moved to Wisconsin in 1855, eventually settling in Oconomowoc (east of Watertown) where he continued to work as a tailor. He was a faithful churchgoer and one of the founders of St. Paul's Lutheran Church in Oconomowoc.

Emil Honerjaeger had the local reputation of having once been a professor, but in Watertown became a tinsmith. Otto Linde followed a similar pattern. He had been both a poet and sculptor in Munich. After settling in Watertown, he opened a bakery and confectionery shop in a corner of the Buena Vista House. In his later years, Linde was a frequent speaker at funerals or at graveside services when prominent German-born Watertownians died. He

Raue paint store
William Raue operated this paint store in Watertown; it was continued by his family for many years. Note the use of *Fraktur* lettering (sometimes called "Gothic" or "German" style) in the large sign. Notice also the feather dusters next to the head of the man atop the ladder at the left.

delivered lengthy and eloquent orations eulogizing the departed member of the community.

Another local Forty-Eighter who acquired craftsman status was William Biebermann. Once a student of the classics at the University of Leipzig, Biebermann became a shoemaker in Watertown. He plied his newfound trade at the Buena Vista House where many of his customers were fellow fugitives. About 1865 he moved to nearby Oconomowoc where he continued work as a shoemaker. He died there in June of 1884 in a drowning accident; he left a wife and six children.

Phillip Schmidt, who had acquired a university education in Germany, became a successful soapmaker in the city. He had an excellent reputation for producing fine quality products. Schmidt's partner for a time was Gustavus Eberle who had been born in far-off Greenland where his father served for forty years as a Moravian missionary.

Henry Pritzlaff followed a somewhat different career path than most of his fellow Forty-Eighters. After leaving Germany in 1855, he came to Milwaukee and operated a hardware store there for nine years. He transferred his business to Watertown in 1864 and continued it until 1877. Pritzlaff then left retailing entirely and became the proprietor of the former Blanchard Flouring Mill. After the mill burned down, he formed a partnership in the commission and grain business known as Pritzlaff & Miller. It had a storage elevator near the Chicago and Northwestern railroad depot on the west side of the city. That business flourished; it also operated a granary in nearby Clyman, six miles north of Watertown. While visiting the Clyman facility in 1888, Pritzlaff took a fall down a flight of steps and suffered such extensive injuries that he died a few days later.

Henry Bassinger was the only member of the artisan/craftsman group who had had formal training as a mason. He was born in Brandenburg, Prussia in 1830, then moved with his parents to Berlin at an early age. It was there he learned his trade. During the Revolution, he became heavily involved with the so-called "liberals." He escaped imprisonment, but in the period of reaction was kept under constant surveillance by the authorities.

Bassinger came to America in 1853, stopped briefly in Milwaukee, but soon came to Watertown to make his home. At the outbreak of the Civil War, he went to Milwaukee and enlisted in Company C, Fifth Wisconsin Volunteer Infantry, a unit also called the Milwaukee Turner Rifles. Bassinger had a long-time association with the Turners.

During the war Bassinger took part in fifteen major battles. He was never wounded, a most remarkable feat considering the proximity with which infantrymen fought in this war. One hot afternoon in July 1863, Bassinger's commanding officer sent him to bring back water from a nearby creek. He filled the buckets he had brought with him, then before returning to his unit, happened to glance upstream. There he saw four badly decaying dead mules lying in the water. At that moment he made an oath never to drink water again. That promise brought Bassinger a measure of notoriety, for he kept it. For the remainder of his life, he drank only coffee, milk, buttermilk, and carbonated drinks such as ginger ale. Occasionally he used beer and wine. But never again water.

Following the war, Bassinger returned to Watertown and resumed his trade as a mason. He followed that calling until he was eighty. He married four times, and outlived each of his wives. Bassinger died in 1932 at the age of 101.

Nordwalde, Westphalia was the birthplace of Joseph Salick on January 3, 1824. He learned his trade as a watchmaker at Steinfurt castle and followed that calling throughout his life.

During the Revolution, Salick served in the German army. He came to the United States soon after, and lived briefly in New Orleans, Cincinnati, and Milwaukee, each the site of a large German population. He moved to Watertown in 1853 where he remained until his death. Salick's decision to leave Germany seems to have stemmed from discontent with the faltering guild system and the lack of economic freedom.

Promptly after making Watertown his new home, Salick opened a watchmaker's shop in the rickety Fischer's block perched above the Rock River. He remained there for a few years, then built his own store on the south side of Main Street, adjacent to the east end of the Main Street bridge. His new shop was almost directly across the street from his old stand. It remained his place of business until his retirement.

Tales of early settlers in America often refer to their working together for the common good. Joseph Salick encountered that type of helpful cooperation in early 1865. On the night of February 19, a devastating fire broke out near his store in Kellogg's Photography Gallery at the southwest corner of First and Main Streets. The five adjacent buildings to the west were all in peril as the flames spread toward them. Salick's store was the furthest of the five from the blaze.

Salick quickly heard of the fire, rushed to the store, and gathered up his most valuable items — gold, jewelry, watches, and the like. He left the scene soon, burdened with his precious inventory. Some of his friends, however, saw that the fire was creeping closer to Salick's store. Determined to help, they broke down the huge plate glass windows and "saved" whatever they could scoop up in their hands. None was aware that the watchmaker himself had

Joseph Salick
During the Revolution, Salick served in the army, "on the other side." He established a watchmaking and jewelry business in Watertown in 1853 that continues in operation today. It is considered the oldest jewelry business in Wisconsin.

already been there and removed what he personally felt needed saving. Henry Mulberger, agent for the Underwriters Insurance Co., made an immediate settlement with Salick.

Salick's skills as a watchmaker were highly regarded by his fellow craftsmen. He earned great praise for the unique clock he built as a showpiece for his store. The entire working mechanism of the clock was housed within its pendulum; the timepiece itself was fashioned after a similar masterpiece which he had helped fabricate back in Germany when he was serving his apprenticeship.

Salick's steady hands and keen eyesight served him well in his craft for many years. When he retired from business in 1910 at the age of eighty-five, he was the oldest active jeweler in the state; he had worked at the bench for seventy years.

Joseph Salick also played an active role in civic affairs. He served as alderman for his ward in 1866, was treasurer of the

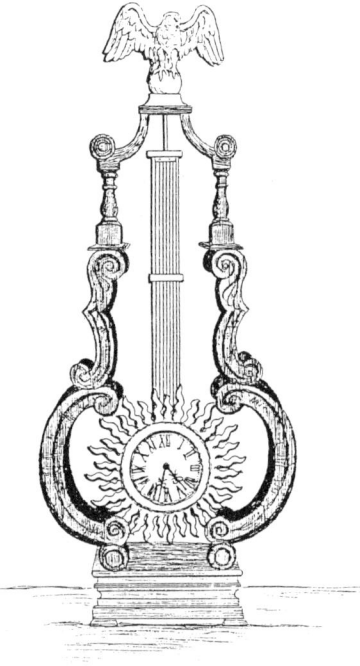

Joseph Salick's amazing clock

As an attraction for customers, Joseph Salick built this unusual clock. All of its working parts are encased behind the dial which is part of the pendulum. The clock is approximately four feet high.

Central Wisconsin Fair Association for a number of years, and held office in several of the benevolent and fraternal organizations to which he belonged. He was also one of the three laymen responsible for founding the local German Catholic church, St. Henry's.

In April of 1864, Salick journeyed back to the fatherland for a visit. Upon his return four months later, he informed the *Weltbürger* that after having lived so many years in Watertown, things were not quite the same in "*das alte Vaterland* (in the old fatherland)." Many factories which made goods for the American market stood empty because of the American Civil War which was still in progress. Cotton and linen products were expensive as a result of the blockade against Southern shipping. And the harvest in Germany would be small because of a cold, raw summer while the wine would turn out bad for the same reason.

Family continuity in the conduct of the business was maintained into the summer of 1988. At that time Salick's great-granddaughter,

Luchsingers — descendants of Joseph Salick
Seated at the right is Margaret Salick Luchsinger, great-granddaughter of Joseph Salick. In 1988 she and her husband retired from the family jewelry business and sold it to others. With her are her son, Steven, and grandson, Joseph. Together they are the fourth, fifth, and sixth generations of the Salick family still living in Watertown.

Margaret Salick Luchsinger and her husband disposed of it to outside interests. Now 136 years old, Salick's continues to be recognized as the oldest jewelry business in Wisconsin.

Another of the skilled artisans who came to Watertown in the aftermath of the Revolution was Daniel Kusel, Sr., born on August 30, 1811 in Grabow near Ludwigsluft, Mecklenburg-Schwerin. As a youth he learned the tinsmith trade, and served as a journeyman in Germany, Denmark, and Russia. By 1836 Kusel had acquired sufficient skills and adequate capital to open his own business as a master tinsmith in Dönitz an der Elbe. The following year he married and soon was the father of four children. Kusel became involved in the Revolution, decided it was untenable to remain in Germany, and in April of 1849 came to America. He brought $3000 in gold with him. After several brief stops en route, he settled in Watertown on June 16, 1849. In July he set up shop in his new homeland as a tinsmith.

Kusel prospered in his undertaking and soon added brass products to his lines of business. Gradually he expanded even further,

Daniel Kusel, Sr.
Kusel was a successful tin and brass goods fabricator in Germany. Forced to flee because of involvement in the Revolution, he came to Watertown in 1849 and began a similar operation. He was also a successful hardware merchant. In 1985, when his concern went out of business, it was considered the oldest hardware store in the state.

first by selling stoves, then by becoming a hardware merchant as well. The tinware that Kusel produced was the foundation upon which he built. One of his earliest undertakings was making intricate wooden forms (although he may have had them built by a local cabinetmaker), then hammering tin into shape over the forms. The resulting panels became part of the facade on the front of a number of local shops and stores. Similarly, other panels were used to make the ornamental ceilings in retail establishments, restaurants, and saloons. A number of these examples of the craftsmanship of a master tinsmith remain in existence in Watertown today where some residents incorrectly perceive them as being cast iron.

Kusel's tinwork included the manufacture and installation of tin roofs for buildings of all types, particularly farm structures. He also turned out rain guttering, downspouts, flashing, and other construction-oriented products. As his business grew and prospered, Kusel added a variety of pieces of labor-saving equipment.

West Avenue, looking west (1886)
D. & F. Kusel was the trade name under which two sons of Daniel Kusel, Sr. continued the family hardware business. It was located on West Avenue, adjacent to the Main Street bridge. This illustration dates from 1886.

These, in turn, helped him to expand and grow even further. Before prosperity came to him, however, Kusel strongly considered moving seventy miles to the north to Oshkosh. He was persuaded to remain in Watertown by fellow Forty-Eighter Carl Schurz.

Kusel was one of the most aggressive of Watertown's early businessmen. His tinware operation continued to expand, and as an offshoot of long experience in fabricating sheet metal, he gradually worked into the manufacture of production equipment for the dairy industry. This portion of Kusel's business continues today as Kusel Equipment Co. When the hardware segment of the Kusel enterprises ceased operations in 1985, it was termed the oldest hardware business in Wisconsin.

A co-founder of the Lutheran church in Watertown, Kusel also helped to establish North Western University in Watertown, a Lutheran seminary. He was instrumental in having the school locate

Die Kaffeemühle **(The Coffee Mill)**
This building stood on the campus of Northwestern College for many years. Since it reminded Watertownians of an old-time coffee mill or grinder, they called this structure by its German name. One of the founders of Northwestern was Forty-Eighter Daniel Kusel, Sr.

in Watertown rather than Milwaukee. The name of the seminary changed in 1910 to Northwestern College. On a number of occasions, Kusel either contributed funds or loaned them to the school when it was faced with financial problems. He was a charter member of its board of directors and served long as its president. In recognition of his many special efforts on its behalf, Kusel was named Northwestern's first honorary director.

When Daniel Kusel, Sr. died on February 22, 1905, he was mourned as one of the city's most respected citizens. He had earned that recognition as a progressive businessman, a devoted churchman, and a Watertownian who had left his mark.

Grocers and Provisioners

While the artisan/craftsman group was comprised of skilled handworkers who had learned their trades in Europe, or occasionally acquired them out of economic necessity in America, prior training was not a requisite to become a grocer or merchant.

Louise Kusel
Miss Kusel's family continued the Kusel businesses in Watertown for many decades. She is the last descendant of her family still living in the city.

Embarking on such a career required more fortitude than any other quality (although a nominal financial base was certainly a necessity as well). The local Forty-Eighters who became grocers, almost without exception used that calling as a springboard to some other career. One has to speculate that being a grocer provided a way to earn a living while accumulating sufficient capital to embark on some other more meaningful career path.

As has been previously related, Henry Mulberger was a grocer for a short time, then turned to a career in law and other fields. Peter Bodien, once a lawyer in Holstein, decided against that career in America, became a grocer instead, and remained one the rest of his life. Charles Grote had a grocery store for a time after leaving Watertown, and ultimately became a judge. The unpredictable Baron Hugo von Bredow engaged in a variety of money-making ventures during his years in Watertown, including a grocery.

Charles Jacobi, who had studied law in Europe, was a government official in the Bavarian Palatinate at the time of the Revolution, became involved in it, and was held a political prisoner. After his release from confinement, he came to the United States and settled in Watertown in 1855. His first business pursuit in the city was as a

Charles H. Jacobi
Jacobi was a Bavarian official, educated in the classics. After imprisonment for his revolutionary activities, he made his way to Watertown. There he was a "Latin farmer," grocer, liquor wholesaler, bedstead manufacturer, bookkeeper, gas company president.

grocer and provisioner. At the same time he added to his income by working as a bookkeeper for a local wholesale business.

Jacobi transferred his energies in 1858 to a wholesale distillery, then in 1865 entered into a partnership in manufacturing bedsteads. When a company was formed to furnish gaslight in the city, he became its president. Jacobi was well respected in the community and was invariably called "Squire" by his fellow townsmen, a title which may have reflected some previously-held judicial position. On the afternoon of September 18, 1866, while driving a buggy to visit his farm outside the city, Jacobi was struck by cerebral apoplexy and died immediately.

One of the most interesting of the Forty-Eighter émigrés was Wenzel Quis. He was born in Bohemia and served as a government overseer of bridge building in Bohemia, Galacia, and Hungary. During the Revolution, Quis served under the determined Louis Kossuth, a personal friend.

Following his participation in the Revolution, Quis came to the United States and located in Watertown in 1850. He operated a general store in the Bohemian settlement at the east end of the Plank Road bridge (today the Oconomowoc Avenue bridge) until the outbreak of the Civil War. Even though he was now fifty-two years old, Quis promptly enlisted in Captain Ernst Off's squadron of the Third Wisconsin Cavalry. He served as a sergeant and took part in a number of engagements, including the battle of Prairie Grove in Arkansas. After being wounded, he was assigned to a reserve regiment of volunteers in Albany, New York. When his three year enlistment expired in November of 1864, he returned home and for a number of years operated a saloon on Main Street. It was probably in that environment that he acquired a reputation for having "a huge imagination which was inclined to overflow at times."

After he had retired, Quis and his wife received a small measure of fame when they celebrated their seventy-fifth or "diamond" wedding anniversary in 1898. When Quis died on April 23, 1913, he had reached the age of 103; he was considered to be "the oldest living surviving soldier of the late civil war" (although by what measure is unknown).

The most enterprising of Watertown's Forty-Eighters was Leopold Kadish. He was involved in dozens of different undertakings during the eleven years he resided in the city. His basic business was a grocery store near the Plank Road bridge, close to that of Wenzel Quis, but on the opposite side of the river.

From the date of his arrival in the city in 1852, Kadish seemed to be in a perpetual state of exploring or promoting some new business venture. He was a notary public for a time as well as a land agent. He sold "German" fire insurance, whatever that might have been. He had lumber in any quantity and quality, hardware of every type, plus grain bags of every size and shape as well as the freshest plums, Dutch herring, aged Ohio whiskey, hard coal, and more.

Kadish was an incurable promoter; he had multiple ads in almost every issue of the *Anzeiger*, and later, the *Weltbürger*. He began a unique business tradition in Watertown on October 6, 1860 that

Second Street at Main Street (June 1866)
While this illustration supposedly is of Watertown's Fair Day, it is unlikely since the crowd of people is not large enough. The building at the extreme right may have been Charlie Lotz's saloon where the *Turnverein* was formed in 1860.

continues today. Initially it was called *Viehmarkt* or "cattle fair," an open air market held on the city streets. It was also called "Pig Day" by some, and "Pomeranian Ascension Day" by others. Originally *Viehmarkt* was held the second Tuesday of every month except during July and August; it gradually evolved into a monthly affair.

Kadish's enterprising world was crushed by a disastrous fire one night in January of 1862. The fire began in the basement of his store at Third and Main Streets where he was now located. The alarm was sounded and a fire engine quickly arrived together with a bevy of volunteer firefighters. But to no avail, for there was no reservoir available from which the engine could pump water. Within four hours, fire had consumed "the most beautiful business block in the city." The entire inventory of Kadish & Co. was destroyed; it was valued between $10-12,000. For some inexplicable reason, the entire amount of insurance carried by this apparently astute businessman was a paltry $2000.

By September 18 of the same year, Kadish, his wife and five others (the latter probably investors in Kadish's enterprises), were sued. The plaintiff seemingly held a mortgage against the Kadish property on the Plank Road. A court judgment was later entered against Kadish and the others which called for the foreclosure and sale of the mortgaged premises on May 25, 1863 at the Planter's Hotel in Watertown. While the outcome of that action could not be determined, it is assumed that the court's orders were carried out.

Soon after, Leopold Kadish disappeared from the city where virtually nothing was heard from him again. He may have moved to Saint Louis, Missouri, for thirty-five years later the *Weltbürger* reprinted a short mystery written by Kadish for the *Mississippi Blätter* of that city. Kadish, the eternal entrepreneur, had somehow survived.

One of the most dramatic rags-to-riches tales of the Watertown Forty-Eighters was that of Frederick Brandt. Brandt was born November 17, 1821 in Sonneborn, Lippe Detmold. His parents were so poor that he was forced to leave home at a very early age. In doing so, he broke the stringent rules that governed the life of a *colonus*, and may have had to avoid the police.

After a number of years, Brandt surfaced as the "mechanical director" (probably corresponding to the present-day stage manager) for the famed composer Richard Wagner. Wagner was widely known for his "radical" or "visionary" opinions, particularly at the time of the Revolution. He was forced to flee to Switzerland in 1849, and Brandt's close connection with him forced Brandt into exile at the same time.

Frederick Brandt arrived in the United States in 1849. He lived briefly in New Orleans, working there as a yellow fever nurse (although he actually may have aided cholera patients). He moved north after a time to Indianapolis, Indiana, where he worked in a sawmill and acquired a piece of land that today is the site of the capitol of that state. By 1854 Brandt was attracted to Watertown in the heart of "the German Triangle" of Milwaukee, Madison, and Manitowoc. He labored first at clearing land, later acquiring a team of oxen to aid him for the princely sum of $150. He subsequently worked for a time at the steam sawmill in the German Sixth Ward. That employment lasted only briefly, for Brandt acquired a horse

Frederick Brandt
Frederick Brandt originally came from Lippe Detmold. He had been the "mechanical manager" for composer Richard Wagner in Dresden, became a Watertown grocer and later a general store owner. Earlier in America he had been a nurse, sawmill operator, and drayman.

and a two-wheeled cart, and with them he became the first drayman in Watertown. He hauled heavy goods, including furniture, within the city.

In 1863 Brandt became a merchant, a partner in a grocery store with fellow-German Daniel Platz. Their business, known as Platz & Brandt, was located on the north side of Main Street, between North Second and North Third. The firm prospered and in 1865 moved into new quarters on the southeast corner of Third and East Main Streets. Brandt had become a well-regarded businessman. This became apparent in 1864 when he was elected to the city council as an alderman.

By the time that Brandt arrived in Watertown in 1854, the local *Freie Gemeinde* had been in existence for several years. He and his

Buffalo Bill in Watertown

When the legendary plainsman and Indian fighter, "Buffalo Bill" — William F. Cody — came to Watertown with his Wild West show, the entire city turned out to see him. The three horsemen were probably Plains Indians. The Brandt & Abele general store (with the iron staircase) at the top center was a major retailer in the city. It was located at the southeast corner of Third and Main Streets. Frederick Brandt was a co-owner of the establishment.

wife became members of the group almost immediately. Brandt eventually served thirty-seven years as a trustee of that congregation. His wife was a member of its Ladies Aid Society for nearly fifty-four years. For a major portion of that period, and up to the time of her death, she was its president. Her services to the society were so highly regarded that on the fiftieth anniversary of her affiliation, a special testimonial service of the parish was held, and she was presented with a large, illuminated bible as a remembrance. Recognizing their obvious commitment to their parish, it is quite surprising that neither Brandt's name nor that of his wife appear in any of the early records of the *Gemeinde.*

Brandt retired from active business in 1887, although he continued to retain a financial interest in his firm. The following year the firm acquired a new name, Brandt & Abele (the latter reflecting partial ownership of its newest partner, Robert Abele). It

Catherine Jean Quirk and her great-grandfather
The late Catherine Quirk and Frederick Brandt are shown in the portion of the double house where he had lived. The other portion was occupied by her grandparents.

was supervised by Brandt's oldest son whom he trained personally for that role. At a later day, when it employed as many as thirty people, the firm carried the name Wm. F. Brandt & Son Co. It was one of the largest retail establishments of any type within the community. The grocery business had been kind to Brandt, who died August 25, 1901.

Brandt's youngest son Edward received national and world-wide acclaim in later years. He was the inventor of the Brandt Automatic Cashier, an ingenious coin-paying machine, and was the founder of a company, now almost a century old, to manufacture it and other money handling products. It continues in Watertown today and bears the Brandt name.

Other Businessmen

One of the local Forty-Eighters who fit no special mold was Charles Paraski. He was born in Prussia, and came to America before the Civil War when he dropped the "von" prefix to his last name. He established himself as a notary, insurance agent, travel agent and money exchange specialist. He later moved to Chicago where he died in 1893. His body was returned to Watertown for burial in the city that had become his new home in America.

Henry Steger was another of the Forty-Eighters who did not fit any special job sector. He came from a well-regarded family in Colberg, Pomerania and had acquired engineering training in both Germany and Paris. After serving as an army lieutenant during the Revolution, he came to America in 1854. He was elected county surveyor for several terms. For many years he was the only surveyor in the area, and he drew many of the early maps of the vicinity.

Contributions to the Arts

It was in the arts that the Forty-Eighters made their greatest contributions to the Watertown community. The first significant history of the city was written in 1868 by Henry Colonius and titled "Geschichte von Watertown, nach mündlichen Überlieferungen

(History of Watertown, in the Oral Tradition)." Earlier efforts had stopped far short of Colonius's enterprising work which ran serially in twenty-four issues of the weekly *Weltbürger.* Falling back on his earlier experience as a newspaperman, Colonius gathered information from persons who had been actively involved in the various events he recorded. What a disappointment that the book he proposed to develop from the series never materialized. It would have been a major achievement in its time, and a resource for modern day historians.

It is hard to imagine that any settlement of Germans could exist long without a singing group society. Watertown was no exception; the first singing society in the entire state was the *Liedertafel,* founded in 1847.

Other musical groups were founded in 1860 and 1861 by Frederick Hoeper and Emil C. Gaebler. Gaebler's singers were called the

Concordia Opera House
The Concordia Musical Society was founded in 1862 by Forty-Eighter Emil C. Gaebler. It was the major choral group in the city for many years. Its opera house was opened in 1888; today it is the home of the local Elks lodge.

Philharmonic Society, and the two organizations consolidated in the fall of 1861 under Gaebler's guidance. Following an internal dispute, a new entity was formed on July 12, 1862 with Gaebler as its leader. It was formally known as the Concordia Musical Society, but within the community was invariably called "the Concordia."

The Concordia was actually a *Männerchor* or *Männergesangverein*, a men's chorus or men's singing society. On occasion it was termed the *Musikverein* (music society). Under Gaebler's leadership it became extremely popular, for it presented a wide variety of music. Women were occasionally invited to take part. In the latter half of the nineteenth century, the populace (including patrons from miles around) heard oratorios, operas, concerts, and operettas which were frequently performed in German. Among the works performed were Josef Haydn's *Creation* and "The Song of the Bell" by Romberg, *The Daughter of the*

Concordia Island

The Concordia *Verein*, the local German singing society, bought Tivoli island in 1874 and gave it their own name. They erected a huge pavilion, planted 2,000 trees, and made it a major recreation center of the city.

Regiment, and *The Magic Flute.* In the presentation of *The Magic Flute,* Gaebler and Phillip Schmidt were among the male leads, while David Blumenfeld's wife and a daughter-in-law of William Wiggenhorn played two of the female roles. When kettledrums were required for the presentation of *Creation,* one was made by a local coppersmith from an old thirty-five gallon brewing kettle that was once part of Charles Ducasse's failed brewery.

The Concordia grew into a widely respected singing society under Gaebler's leadership. It became an active participant in gatherings of the Northwestern *Sängerbund,* a group of which he co-founded. Gaebler was the leader at four of the festivals of the *Sängerbund.* In addition, its *Sängerfest* was held in Watertown three times, in 1867, 1875, and in 1885.

The Concordia generally had from thirty to thirty-five members. After fire destroyed its meeting place in the old *Freie Gemeinde* building, the membership voted to build its own facility. When the Concordia Opera House opened on June 23, 1888, the first piece

Sängerfest **returns in 1885** After two prior meetings in Watertown, the Northwest *Sängerfest* returned in 1885. The display of evergreens and garlands mark this as a typical German event.

74

performed on its stage was the baritone aria from *Tannhäuser,* "O du mein holder Abendstern (Evening Star)." It was sung by *Verein* president Edward J. Brandt, son of Forty-Eighter Frederick Brandt. One wonders if the association of his father back in Germany with the aria's composer Richard Wagner influenced his choice of that selection.

The Concordia did not limit its programs to performances by its own members. For example, on April 19, 1887 it presented a spectacular evening's entertainment by the famed P. C. Gilmore and his "incomparable band." Gilmore, it will be recalled, was the enterprising bandmaster who preceded John Philip Sousa in receiving widespread acclaim in the United States.

Turners honor *Sängerfest*
When the Northwest *Sängerfest* was held in Watertown in 1875, the local *Turnverein* erected a huge triumphal arch in honor of the occasion. Notice the greeting in German at the top of the arch and the American flags above it.

The Concordia had one rather unusual tradition. When one of its group died, surviving members of the society would gather at the graveside for the burial service and sing two or three farewell songs. On occasion, an eloquent funeral oration would also be delivered. The Watertown Forty-Eighters who are known to have belonged to the Concordia were David Blumenfeld, Emil C. Gaebler, Phillip Schmidt, Henry Bieber, and Frederick Hoeper. A number of sons of Forty-Eighters were also affiliated with the *Verein*.

The director of another of Watertown's early singing societies was Louis Hillmantel, once a schoolteacher in Germany. He had owned a piano in the old country and had retained the tuning key which had come with it when he came to America. This "tuning key" was probably a forerunner of today's "tuning hammer," the device used to adjust the tension of the strings, although it may have been a "tuning fork."

One day Hillmantel learned that the piano — the only one in town — used by the daughter of one of the local Yankee innkeepers required tuning. His financial state at the time was desperate, and even though he knew nothing about properly tuning a piano, he confidently made his way to the inn. Upon arriving, the landlord asked Hillmantel what he wanted. Neither man knew more than a few words in the other's language. Suddenly the little ex-schoolteacher was struck by a brilliant idea to explain his presence, and showed the innkeeper his tuning key and wire pliers. The landlord, who had suffered all night long with an excruciating toothache, immediately concluded that his visitor was a dentist. Without any delay, he immediately dropped into a nearby armchair, tossed back his head, opened his mouth, and after pointing out the aching tooth, gestured to the surprised and confused music director to get on with the job.

History fails to record the conclusion of this comedy of errors, whether the tooth was pulled, or whether the piano was tuned. What is known, however, is that Hillmantel later left Watertown with a circus as its calliope player. He subsequently found his way to Milwaukee where he died after serving there as a high school principal.

Physical culture was also important to Watertown's German immigrants. In early August of 1860, a group of enterprising young Germans led by Ernst Grossmann gathered in a back room of Charlie Lotz's saloon at the northeast corner of Second and East Washington Streets (today's Market Street). After lengthy discussion, they formed the *Unabhängiger Turnverein von Watertown* (the Independent Gymnastic Society of Watertown). Grossmann was elected First Speaker (president). Among the founders and early members of the Turners were Leopold Kadish, Charles M. Ducasse, Phillip Schmidt, and Emil Rothe. Other Forty-Eighters who joined the organization at a later date were Henry Bieber, Otto Linde, and Henry Colonius.

The Watertown Turners pursued physical fitness, concentrating on the training of young men beginning at the age of fifteen. There was also a singing group, a theatrical section, and a select few specialists who performed on the parallel bars. Within a year, the Turners put on their first theatrical production. The event was held at Cole's Hall on February 24, 1861.

Soon after the outbreak of the Civil War, Company E of the 20th Wisconsin Volunteer Infantry was formed in Watertown. The majority of its members were Turners, and the unit was often referred to as "the Watertown Turner" company. Its company commander for a time was Captain Fred Kusel, son of Forty-Eighter Daniel Kusel.

During the war, the Turners were inactive. After peace returned in 1865, the club resumed its activities. Within a few short years, the *Verein* decided to build its own facility which was erected on the vacant circus grounds between Fourth and Fifth Streets, south of Jefferson Street. The new three-story *Turn-Halle* opened on December 11 and 12, 1869. On opening night, an audience of 1300 people filled the auditorium to see *The Magic Flute*. For a number of years, the Turners presented a program every two weeks during the winter, alternating with events put on by the Concordia.

In the years before the Concordia and the Turners existed, the energetic Germans also formed a theatrical group. Joseph Engelmann, Theodore Bernhard, and Dr. Christian Fischer were the directors. Henry Steger served as stage manager and Frederick

Hoeper as music director. Steger was also one of the scenery painters.

The most prominent of Watertown's Forty-Eighters active in the arts was Emil C. Gaebler. Gaebler was born September 30, 1828 in Eisenberg, Saxony-Altenburg. He had hoped to follow a career in theology, but his involvement at the time of the Revolution in trying to free a political prisoner made him suspect. He had previously been warned by the local Board of Education regarding his outspoken comments on "freedom." His planned theological career was ruined.

While avoiding the authorities by hiding in the home of Dr. Carl Alfred Douai, Gaebler became acquainted with a sister of the doctor's wife, the Baroness Charlotte Bertha von Beust. The young couple fell in love, and were married on June 3, 1849. Within a few weeks, the newlyweds sailed to the United States.

Gaebler's efforts to find work in New York were unsuccessful. He applied for jobs as a teacher, piano tuner, pharmacist's assistant, bookbinder, even a salesman. He finally took work as the business

Emil C. Gaebler
Gaebler was a talented musician who founded the Concordia *Sängerverein*, or singing society, and was its leader for many years. He also manufactured both organs and melodeons.

manager for a cabinetmaker. That employment lasted only briefly, for he found a job much more to his liking as a teacher at Danbury College in Danbury, Connecticut. As a condition of employment, he agreed to shave off his mustache.

Within a matter of months, Gaebler abandoned his role as a languages and music teacher, and set himself up as a private music instructor, giving both piano and voice lessons. Ill health forced him to leave Connecticut in 1856. A change of climate had been prescribed, so Gaebler and his wife moved to Lake Mills, Wisconsin, twelve miles southwest of Watertown. There they were able to join other members of his family. He established a hardware business that was quite successful.

In 1858 the young couple came to Watertown. The recently founded St. Mark's Lutheran church was in need of an organist. Gaebler took the position. Within a short time he undertook a further challenge, the manufacture of both parlor and church organs. For a while he also built melodeons, but dropped that product line in the face of stiff price competition. He also opened a music store on North Fourth Street for the sale of musical instruments and supplies.

Mrs. Emil C. Gaebler (Baroness Charlotte von Beust)
Emil Gaebler's wife was one of the small number of nobility who came to Watertown in the aftermath of the Revolution. She was an accomplished vocalist and shared her husband's interest in music.

The intense love of music shown by both Gaebler and his wife (she had an excellent voice and had received extensive formal training in Europe) attracted many of the local citizenry to their home. It was the musical headquarters of the city.

During his years in Watertown, Gaebler was an advocate of education. He served on the local school board for two terms of two years each, in 1876 and 1878. He was a particularly strong proponent of the free textbook system, and aided in having that program initiated in Watertown.

Gaebler founded the Concordia Music Society in 1862 and co-founded the Northwest *Sängerbund* in 1866. In 1881 he received an invitation to take charge of the singing societies of La Crosse, Wisconsin, which was already a much larger city than Watertown. He moved there and remained until his retirement in 1882. In 1886 moved to Milwaukee.

Gaebler and his wife had nine children, four of whom died as youngsters. Their daughter Sophie won wide recognition, for she had an exceptional voice and was acclaimed as a pianist. She had studied under the composer and performer Franz Liszt in Europe. In her later years, Sophie was a widely sought music teacher in Milwaukee.

Following Bertha's death on January 22, 1889, Gaebler remarried. His second wife was Catherine Juessen of Watertown, the widow of Jacob Juessen, Carl Schurz's uncle and one-time postmaster of the city. Emil C. Gaebler died in Milwaukee on April 9, 1898. His body was brought to Watertown for burial. When he was laid to rest in Oak Hill Cemetery, the six pallbearers were members of the Concordia which had meant so much to him. One was fellow Forty-Eighter Emil Honerjaeger. And following the tradition which he had undoubtedly helped to create, the Concordia sang its farewell songs after the funeral oration.

In appraising the artistic contributions of his fellow-countrymen in his "Geschichte von Watertown," Colonius observed that "the arts flourished also among the businesses, and made the Germans advance in the respect and goodwill of the Americans by furthering the arts."

The Military and The War of Rebellion

One of the contributions made by the Watertown Forty-Eighters to their new homeland was participation in military affairs. Prior to the Civil War, during the period when it was the second largest community in Wisconsin, Watertown had two militia units. The Germans were dominant in both the rifle company and the artillery detachment. Only one of the Forty-Eighters was known to be a member of either. Henry Mulberger served for a time as first lieutenant in the artillery company, and later was its commanding officer as a captain. Both units were dissolved in 1858.

It was not surprising that Ernst Off chose to join the Union Army at the outset of the Civil War. His father had been a physician in the French army, and Off himself served several years as a lieutenant in the same army, including two years of duty in Algiers. He came to America in 1849, stayed several months in Virginia, then moved to Watertown in 1850. For about two years he farmed west of the city, then moved into the community where he operated a cigar store for a time.

In 1853 he was elected city marshal. This was at a time when cholera took the lives of many. Late in the summer of 1853, the disease was so widespread that six to eight funerals were held each day. In several instances, entire families were wiped out. Although cholera victims were generally shunned or avoided, Off moved among the sick to give whatever assistance he could. He aided in the removal of the dead and helped to arrange for their burial. These demonstrations of courage, at great risk to his own health, won him strong admiration among his fellow citizens.

Off was commissioned a captain of the Union army on December 3, 1861 and the following January was called to active duty. He was made the company commander of Company K, Third Wisconsin Cavalry, and served in Missouri, Kansas, and Arkansas and took part in the battle of Prairie Grove in Arkansas. Injured when his horse fell on him, Off was hospitalized for a time in Saint Louis. He was mustered out of service in 1865. Soon after returning to Watertown, Off again became city marshal. In the fall of 1872, he was elected sheriff of Jefferson County. He moved to Jefferson to assume that position; he died there on March 16, 1874.

As related earlier, Wenzel Quis, friend of the Hungarian revolutionary leader, Louis Kossuth, enlisted in the Third Wisconsin Cavalry at the age of fifty-one. He fought in two major engagements, and was wounded.

When the impressive career of Carl Schurz is discussed, his military service is sometimes overlooked or down-played because of his many other accomplishments. Yet Schurz had a very active role in the Civil War of the United States.

When the war broke out, Schurz was determined to be a part of it. He was keenly aware of the advantages of having a military background as part of his overall career goals. Moreover, Schurz felt that he was something of an expert in military affairs. Yet his only prior military experience was while serving as a lieutenant in an artillery unit of the revolutionary command in Germany. He was lightly wounded in his first engagement, a skirmish in Bruchsal, and saw minor action later at Ubstadt.

Schurz's strong support of Lincoln quickly brought him a commission as colonel; he was ultimately promoted to major general, the highest rank then existing in the United States Army. Schurz was recognized as being a "political" general whose commission was a reflection of his valuable service to the Republican party in the 1860 presidential campaign. As might be expected, Schurz was not too popular among professional soldiers, especially the West Point graduates over whom he sometimes held command.

Despite the attention he attracted as a "political" general, he gave a good overall account of himself in battle. He commanded troops that took part in the second battle of Bull Run, as well as Chancellorsville, Gettysburg, and Chattanooga. His actions at Chancellorsville, however, came under criticism where his troops were charged with cowardice.

The Remarkable Career of Carl Schurz

Carl Schurz, his wife, his parents and sisters came to Watertown late in the winter of 1855; they arrived on March 3. Schurz's uncle

Jacob Juessen, once a cloth merchant and the mayor of Jülich in Germany, already lived in the city. Schurz was caught up in the heady expectations of these times when many people were convinced Watertown was to become a great railroad center. He bought an eighty-nine acre farm on the northwest side of the city in September of 1855 from John Jackson. It was located on Oak Grove Street (today an extension of North Church Street), adjacent to the Rock River Valley Union Railroad and overlooked Silver Creek.

It was on this property that Schurz built a home for his wife and children that was completed in the fall of 1856. He called the structure "a modest but pretty comfortable cottage," while townspeople considered it a "villa" or "small castle" or "chateau." The house was a hideous example of architecture, badly overdone with rococo ornamentation. It was situated in the midst of a rather large grove of trees. Two concentric paths near the front of the house may have been riding paths for the children.

Carl and Margarethe Schurz
Carl and Margarethe — she was called Gredel by her husband — were married in London in July 1852. In September of that same year they arrived in New York to begin a new life. They came to Watertown in 1855; it was their legal residence for eleven years.

83

The entire "farm" as Schurz sometimes called it was located within the city limits, and it was operated as a farm. Part of Schurz's "household" in 1860 were Edward Kruger, his wife Johannah, and their children Frederick and Herman. Kruger apparently was the day-to-day farmer who actually tended to the livestock and the fields. The Schurz's also employed two servants, Ellen Flavin of Massachusetts, and Mina Humbolt from Prussia.

While the farm was purchased in part to be the site of a family home, Schurz was confident that he could make a handsome profit by subdividing part of it into residential plots. He had the parcel staked out; in doing so, "C. Schurz's addition" to the city of Watertown was created. After the subdivision had been established, the confident entrepreneur sat back and waited for the money to start rolling in. It did not; the entire scheme was a financial disaster. The Schurz farm was sold at a sheriff's sale on Saturday, March 30,

Schurz's home in Watertown
Carl and Margarethe's home was far removed from the business district, yet was within the city limits. This location probably accounts for the heavy stand of trees around it. Fire destroyed the house in 1915.

1867 to one James K. Hyde of Vermont for a mere $5000. Schurz had paid about $10,000 for it originally (perhaps slightly less), and had signed a mortgage for $8500. The home and at least two out-buildings that were there would have increased the value of the of the property materially. In telling of Schurz and the sale, the *Weltbürger* concluded, *"Er ist ein besserer Zeitungsschreiber wie Farmer* [he is a better newspaperman than a farmer]."

In his earliest months in Watertown, Schurz lived an idyllic life. He and Emil Rothe went hunting together for prairie chickens, snipe, and quail. On occasion an "operatic concert" was performed by Milwaukee artists who came to the city, and Schurz attended. There were small parties, balls, even a masquerade. The Schurz home was considered the "rendezvous" for Watertown's elite.

Schurz would stop on occasion at the Buena Vista House to shoot billiards with friends, or he would visit one of his favorite local saloons, including those of fellow Forty-Eighters Henry Bieber, Jacob Karst, and M. D. Marx.

Carl Schurz as a young man

The idealistic, energetic young Schurz — and many of his fellow dissidents — often wore the black, red, and gold colors of the Revolution inside their coats as either a cockade or sash.

All of this was a prelude to Schurz's becoming involved in the actual political process prevailing in the United States. In 1857, when an alderman's vacancy occurred in Watertown's heavily German Fifth Ward where he lived, Schurz ran for the post and was elected by a vote of 88 to 26 over his opponent, J. Baumann. Emil Rothe was picked as an alderman in the same election. Even though he was a very strong Republican, Schurz struck up a friendship with the editor of the *Watertown Democrat*, Daniel W. Ballou. Prior to each meeting of the city council, Schurz would come to Ballou's office, where together they would go over the resolutions or proposals he expected to make at the meeting. Ballou helped his new friend get each of his ideas into the proper form and in the appropriate English wording so that "everything [would] appear correct and business-like." This approach, in turn, gave Schurz another method of improving his written and spoken English, and added to his insight into the workings of the American system of government at the local level.

Schurz soon became fluent in English. His American and Irish colleagues in the city council expressed surprise that this " 'green' young Dutchman" had acquired such a strong command of the language as compared to the other German councilmen who rarely came out with any words in English other than "aye" or "nay."

Schurz's Triumphant Return to Watertown

The biggest and warmest welcome that Carl Schurz ever received in Watertown occurred in the fall of 1872. The announcement was made in the local press that Schurz would return to the city on Thursday, September 19 to speak on behalf of Horace Greeley in his campaign for the presidency of the United States. Greeley was the candidate of the Liberal Republican party in opposition to Ulysses S. Grant who was seeking reelection. A further drawing card for the grand celebration was that Emil Rothe, now living in Cincinnati, had agreed to return to Watertown to appear on the platform with Schurz and speak as well.

The *Weltbürger* and the *Democrat* touted the homecoming with vigor. Inasmuch as Schurz had abandoned his long association with the Republican party to side with the Liberal Republicans, the *Watertown Republican* predictably gave modest recognition to the occasion.

The excitement generated by the announcement was all the more unusual because Schurz was not well liked in Watertown. He was considered *"ein verdammter Republikaner* (a damned Republican)"* in a city that was overwhelmingly populated by Democrats. Moreover, Schurz and his wife were not churchgoers; this was anathema to the "churchy" Watertownians.

On Wednesday, September 18, the vanguard of the welcoming committee traveled to Milton Junction, about thirty-five miles to the south of Watertown. There Schurz and Rothe were each greeted by separate delegations of the welcoming group, to be escorted in honor back to Watertown.

The train eventually departed, first backtracking to Janesville for a short stop, then proceeding northward to Jefferson. A crowd

Schurz plays the piano in the White House
When Carl Schurz was the Secretary of the Interior (1877-81), he was invited with Margarethe to the White House. There he played the piano for President Rutherford B. Hayes and his guests.

reported to be between 600 and 1,000 people greeted the train there on barely one hour's notice; apparently this was an unexpected stop. It may have happened at Schurz's instigation, for as an astute politician he undoubtedly recalled that it was in Jefferson where he had made his first political speech in the United States.

At four o'clock in the afternoon the train finally chugged into Watertown. On its arrival, the German Band broke into stirring music as a huge crowd gathered about. When Schurz finally appeared on the rear platform of the train, a thunderous cheer went up from the throng while a cannon boomed out nearby. The cheers kept ringing out, then recurred when Emil Rothe, an old favorite of Watertowners (the then-popular title for local residents), made his appearance. The guests were escorted to waiting carriages, Schurz going to the home of his friend, Henry Mulberger, while Rothe went to the homes of some of his old acquaintances.

There were two unusual "reunions" for Schurz in this welcome back to Watertown. The first was his reunion with Emil Rothe on their journey to the city. While they had been friends both in Germany and in Watertown, they had a bitter falling out when Schurz suspected that Rothe had slurred him some time earlier through an article in the Beaver Dam (Wisconsin) *Democrat*. The story — later proved to be a blatant lie — attempted to charge that Schurz was a Prussian spy whose property had never been confiscated back in Germany.

The second "reunion" was with the chairman of the grand celebration, D. W. Ballou, editor of the *Democrat*. Earlier in 1872, Ballou had recalled in his paper an event that had happened in 1857. Schurz at that time was a candidate for the lieutenant governor's post of Wisconsin on the Republican ticket. Ballou pointed out in his paper that Schurz was not yet a citizen, and that he would not qualify to preside over the state senate if he were elected. "His anger and indignation knew no bounds," wrote Ballou, adding that Schurz considered the disclosure to be "a spiteful and malicious attack." Ballou argued in his 1872 article that he believed his actions to be "fair political warfare, a candidate's eligibility and fitness having always been regarded as open to discussion."

The sun rose bright and warm on the morning of the nineteenth. Schurz found time to journey out to his former home in the Fifth Ward and he paid a brief visit on old friends and neighbors. Wherever he stopped, a table filled with food and drink had been set in his honor; he sampled at every location he visited. Rothe attempted to go into the city to renew old friendships, but the crowd that quickly assembled literally besieged him and made it impossible for him to get through the streets.

The first out-of-town group of supporters arrived in the city at 9:00 A.M., but as noon approached, the crowd increased dramatically in size. At least seventeen nearby cities and villages were represented with delegations, with one of the larger groups coming from Columbus where Schurz's sister, Antonie (Mrs. Edmund Juessen) lived.

The parade formed at 1:00 P.M., led by Miller's German Band and the Watertown Cornet Band. It marched to Henry Mulberger's home on the west side of the river from which Schurz was escorted to a waiting carriage. Then, led by 100 riders and escorted by at least five bands, the entire crowd moved through the city streets to the Public Square (today Veteran's Memorial Park), between Third and Fourth Streets in the First Ward. A throng of between 7,000 and 8,000 persons had gathered.

The formal program began at 2:00 P.M. when Schurz was introduced to the throng. Applause continued in wave after wave until he finally quieted it by repeatedly waving his hat. He then launched into a two hour address in English marked by "unrivaled and sustained eloquence." Dr. William F. Whyte, a local physician and well-respected historian as well as a backer of President Grant was present. He later wrote, "... as a supporter of Grant, I must confess that while listening to his speech he nearly took me off my feet. It was a terrific arraignment of Grant's administration; but I had to admit to its truthfulness. I was comforted by only one circumstance — he did not say a word in favor of Horace Greeley. He denounced with all the eloquence at his command the faults and blunders of Grant, and at the end of any period his refrain was, 'My friends, if you do not like this, then range yourselves under the banner on which the name of Horace Greeley is inscribed.' " After

Schurz had concluded his remarks, Emil Rothe spoke in German for half an hour. His remarks were repeatedly interrupted by applause.

When the afternoon program was completed, the speakers returned to their accommodations. Following dinner, another parade formed at 7:00 P.M. at the railroad station at the foot of Fifth Street where ten cars of visitors from Milwaukee had arrived. The long column of marchers then inched its way through the city along Main Street. It passed under a triumphal arch bedecked with ever-greens and flowers which was topped by a huge wreath reading, "Welcome Carl Schurz." Six hundred flickering torches carried by marchers lit the night while numerous homes and businesses were decorated with sparkling Chinese lanterns. The mass of enthusiasts finally reached Turner Hall. One guess placed over 2,000 people inside the auditorium plus another 3,000 outside who had been unable to gain entry. Rothe spoke first to the assembly, "with his accustomed fervor and brilliancy." Accounts are contradictory about which language he used. Then Schurz followed, with a shorter message than in the afternoon. This time he addressed his listeners in German.

Schurz and his sister
Late in life Schurz enjoyed the quiet surroundings at Bolton Landing, N. Y., with his sister Antonie (Mrs. Edmund Jüssen).

About 11:00 P.M. the gatherings inside and outside Turner Hall finally dispersed. Schurz caught a night train to Chicago, on his way to Fort Wayne, Indiana where he was to speak the following Saturday. Rothe's departure was not noted. Schurz's return to Watertown for this gala event is believed to have been the last time he visited the city. It had been his legal residence for eleven years.

In a brief aside to its report, "The Schurz Meeting," the *Republican* noted that Christian Schroeder, the city's coffin builder and undertaker, had held an umbrella over Schurz's head as he spoke during the afternoon rally to shield the Senator from the scorching sun. It added that a local Irishman questioned whether Schroeder was "playing smart," presumably in the hopes of having Schurz, Horace Greeley, and the other Liberal Republicans as "customers" after their anticipated demise in the November elections.

On June 3, 1983, seventy-seven years after his death, the United States Postal Service issued a commemorative stamp honoring Carl Schurz as part of its Great American Series. This stamp is the only one known to have been issued to honor a Forty-Eighter in any country. The first place of issue chosen by the Postal Service was the best recognized "home town" of Schurz in America, Watertown.

Carl Schurz stamp
The most widely recognized Forty-Eighter who came to the United States from Germany was Carl Schurz. When the Great American series of U. S. postage stamps was created in 1983, Schurz was honored by being pictured on the 4¢ denomination. The first place of issue was in the city best recognized as his home in America, Watertown.

The Bubble Bursts

Watertown's dynamic growth was abruptly ended by the Panic of 1857. The city had underwritten huge bond issues to support railroad expansion; the panic caused every railroad project in Wisconsin to collapse including those in Watertown. While red bankruptcy flags hung outside dozens of local businesses, no Watertown Forty-Eighter is known to have been affected in that way. Moreover none has been identified as having left the city as a direct result of the Panic. The city's population dropped by almost fifty percent within three years to 5,302, and Watertown's growth was negligible for almost seventy-five years.

Ebenezer Cole, one of the city's earliest settlers and a Yankee, claimed in later years that "if it had not been for the Germans with the capital [they brought with them] and the[ir] industriousness...[it would have been] impossible for us Americans to hold our own...." Henry Colonius, in his detailed "Geschichte von Watertown", gave little credit to the Forty-Eighters for the development of the city. But the impact of the Forty-Eighters on Watertown is glowingly described by Ralph Blumenfeld. On the first page of his autobiography, *Home Town*, he tells of the Watertown he knew, as "a Mecca," "Utopia in the West," "this Athens-to-be," "this Storybook City." He attributes much of this heady atmosphere to the presence of the Forty-Eighters, noting that "in this still primitive atmosphere [these refugees of the revolution] proceeded to develop a community which has, perhaps, not been equaled in the modern history of civic intercourse." The truth seems to lie somewhere between this flattering assessment and the curt dismissal of Colonius.

None of the Watertown Forty-Eighters appears to have had strong expectations of a successful revolution in Germany, nor do any appear to have planned for such an eventuality. There apparently were no clandestine meetings to discuss "the next revolution." While several went on to live relatively undistinguished lives and a few died in impoverished circumstance, only one (Kadish) had the misfortune to undergo bankruptcy. None died of the dreaded cholera that hung over the city during most of 1849 through 1854. Even though suicide was not uncommon in the city, no Watertown

Forty-Eighter chose that alternative to trying times in America. A handful of Forty-Eighters sought elective or appointive offices and retained them. This may have been a conscious effort toward job security, without the hazards of competing in the conventional business world. Only two of Watertown's freedom-seekers chose to return to Germany.

Perhaps the strongest contribution made by the Watertown Forty-Eighters was their enthusiastic commitment to education, together with their eagerness and willingness to be part of the elective process of government. As a group they had a large measure of self-reliance or, perhaps, self-sufficiency. They made their commitment to come to America and to Watertown; the majority were confident that they would not fail. Their determination to succeed (or possibly it was innate stubbornness), helped to set standards for the other residents of their city. These values served them well in their lifetimes, and to a large measure, were carried on for over a century.

It was the involvement of Watertown's Forty-Eighters in a great revolutionary process that brought them to the United States. Though they accepted most of the laws and customs of their new homeland, they were active in efforts to make it more democratic, which included their fight against slavery. They lived within the law and had no further need to be involved in revolution. They must be judged successful, for they accomplished their goals.

APPENDIX A

THE FORTY-EIGHTERS OF WATERTOWN, WISCONSIN

The following one-time residents of Watertown are the persons who have been identified as having had some connection with the events surrounding the Revolution of 1848 in Germany. Their best known occupations in Germany are listed first; those with which they were best associated in the United States follow the semi-colon. The symbol "@" is used to indicate an approximate date.

Louis Baehr: university student, estate manager; restaurant owner.
  1814 — Kassel
  Mar. 12, 1870 — Watertown

Henry Bassinger: mason; soldier, mason.
  Sept. 8, 1830 — Brandenburg, Prussia
  May 21, 1932 — Watertown

Theodore Bernhard: university student, private tutor; educator, state assemblyman.
  June 17, 1820 — Berlin
  June 27, 1879 — Watertown

Adolph Beurhaus: unknown; hotel keeper, saloon owner.
  1810
  Sept. 26, 1861 — Watertown

Henry Bieber: university student; saloon owner, city clerk.
  Jan. 24, 1827 — Zweibrücken, Rhenish Bavaria
  Feb. 28, 1904 — Watertown

William Biebermann: university student; shoemaker.
  @1831
  June 21, 1881 — Oconomowoc, Wisconsin

David Blumenfeld: soldier, printer; printer, newspaperman.
Feb. 13, 1828 — Creglingen, Württemberg
Sept. 25, 1905 — Watertown

Peter Bodien: lawyer; newspaperman, grocer.
Feb. 24, 1806 — Holstein
Mar. 20, 1877 — Watertown

_____ **Boenig**: artillery officer; unknown.
Unknown
Unknown

Frederick Brandt: theater mechanical director; grocer, general
store owner.
Nov. 17, 1821 — Sonneborn, Lippe Detmold
Aug. 25, 1901 — Watertown

Hugo von Bredow: baron, cavalry officer; farmer, hotel
keeper.
Sept. 22, 1824 — Rathenow, Brandenburg
Mar. 23, 1904 — Watertown

Henry Colonius: student; commission merchant, county judge.
Mar. 12, 1831 — Wächtersbach, Hesse
Aug. 21, 1896 — Jefferson, Wisconsin

Paul Creydt: chemistry professor; farmer.
Unknown
Unknown

Rev. Max de Beck: military chaplain; Catholic parish priest.
@1821 — Hungary
Apr. 25, 1879 — Sun Prairie, Wisconsin

Charles M. Ducasse: civil engineer; hotel owner, surveyor.
1815 — Nancy, France
June 14, 1876 — Watertown

Dr. Clemens T. Eger: physician; physician.
Apr. 15, 1828 — Germany
June 1, 1921 — Watertown

Joseph Engelmann: theologian; newspaperman.
Unknown
Unknown

Dr. Carl R. Feld, Sr.: university student, soldier; pharmacist, physician.
Apr. 5, 1816 — Kreuznach, Prussia
Apr. 8, 1887 — Watertown

Dr. Christian H. Fischer: university student; physician.
@1811 — Hannover
1876

Emil C. Gaebler: student; music director, organ manufacturer.
Sept. 30, 1828 — Eisenberg, Saxony-Altenburg
April 9, 1898 — Milwaukee

Franz Graefe: university student; distillery owner.
Unknown
Unknown, presumed Germany

Ernst Grossmann: university medical student, postmaster; cigar manufacturer, land agent.
Mar. 9, 1821 — Battenberg, Hesse
Apr. 9, 1885 — Watertown

Charles H. Grote: university student; distillery owner, county judge.
Mar. 1, 1829 — Rhenish Prussia
Sept. 9, 1909 — Mauston, Wisconsin

Frederick Hermann: student; saloon and beer garden owner, local politician.
June 21, 1819 — Adelsheim, Baden
Mar. 14, 1896 — Watertown

Louis Hillmantel: schoolteacher; music director, high school principal.
Unknown
Late 1890s — Milwaukee, Wisconsin

Frederick Hoeper: business manager to nobility; music teacher and director.
@1820 — Hanover
Mar. 10, 1892 — Watertown

Emil Honerjaeger: professor; tinsmith.
Unknown
Unknown

Charles H. Jacobi: law student, government official; farmer, bedstead manufacturer.
@1809
Sept. 18, 1866 — Watertown

Ignatz Jahna: soldier; farmer.
1828 — Landkrone, Austria
Sept. 30, 1899 — Richwood, Wisconsin

Leopold J. Kadish: soldier; merchant, lumber dealer.
Unknown
Unknown

Jacob Karst: unknown; farmer, saloon owner.
1806 — Stromberg near Bingen
May 7, 1877 — Chicago

John L. Kube: judge; justice of the peace, deputy sheriff.
Nov. 25, 1816 — Poland
Unknown

Daniel Kusel, Sr.: tin and brass artisan; manufacturer, hardware merchant.
Aug. 30, 1811 — Grabow near Ludwigsluft, Mecklenberg-Schwerin
Feb. 22, 1905 — Watertown

Georg Hugo Licht: law student; art and music teacher.
1809 — Fraustadt, Posen
Mar. 2, 1885 — Watertown

Otto Linde: poet, sculptor; baker, confectioner.
Unknown
Unknown

Hermann (von) Lindemann: soldier, newspaperman; newspaperman.
Unknown
Nov. 26, 1871 — Jefferson City, Missouri

M. D. Marx: Catholic priest; farmer, saloon operator.
@1803
Dec. 6, 1874 — Juneau, Wisconsin

Bernard Miller: student; cigar manufacturer, flouring mill owner.
@1825 — Berlin
Unknown

Henry Mulberger: woolen goods manufacturing employee;
lawyer, local politician.
June 10, 1824 — Speyer, Rhenish Palatinate
Jan. 19, 1896 — Watertown

Ernst Off: soldier; city marshal, county sheriff.
1828 — Lichtenstein, Württemberg
Mar. 16, 1874 — Jefferson, Wisconsin

Charles J. Palme: unknown; lawyer, newspaperman.
@1817
Sept. 1879 — East Pepperell, Massachusetts

Charles (von) Paraski: unknown; travel agent, insurance agent.
Jan. 5, 1822 — Kamin, Prussia
Aug. 11, 1893 — Chicago

Henry M. Peters: tailor; tailor.
Oct. 8, 1820 — Demmin, Prussia
Jan. 1907 — Oconomowoc, Wisconsin

Edward Pfenniger: estate inspector; justice of the peace.
Unknown
Unknown

Henry Pritzlaff: soldier; hardware merchant, grain and produce
dealer.
Nov. 24, 1824 — Triegloff, Pomerania
Feb. 6, 1888 — Watertown

Wenzel Quis: railroad construction supervisor, soldier; saloon keeper, grocer.
Oct. 10, 1809 — Bohemia
Apr. 23, 1913 — Watertown

Louis W. Ranis: archaeologist; professor, farmer. (Not to be confused with Louis F. Ranis, a cooper, who lived in Watertown at the same time.)
1810 — Rabenhausen, Hesse Darmstadt
Jan. 2, 1896 — La Crosse, Wisconsin

Emil Rothe: university student; newspaperman, lawyer.
Sept. 23, 1826 — Guhrau, Silesia
Apr. 27, 1895 — Cincinnati, Ohio

Joseph Salick: soldier; watchmaker, jeweler.
Jan. 3, 1824 — Nordwalde, Westphalia
Oct. 17, 1910 — Watertown

Phillip Schmidt: analytical chemist; fresco painter, soap maker.
1832 — Prussia
Unknown

_____ Schumann: university student; unknown.
Unknown
Unknown

Carl Schurz: university student; politician, U.S. senator, Secretary of the Interior, newspaperman.
Mar. 2, 1829 — Liblar near Cologne
May 14, 1906 — New York City

Henry Steger: construction engineer, soldier; civil engineer, surveyor.
@1820 — Colburg, Pomerania
Jan. 4, 1867 — Watertown

Joseph Stoppenbach: lawyer, notary; politics, founder of title and abstract business.
July 28, 1800 — Sindlar near Cologne on Rhine, Rhenish Prussia
Jan. 13, 1884 — Jefferson, Wisconsin

Johann G. Strauss: soldier, shoemaker; shoemaker, farmer.
   May 11, 1823 — Sillenbach near Stuttgart,
   Württemberg
   Nov. 6, 1900 — Watertown

Adolf Strodtmann: university student; author, translator.
   Apr. 24, 1829 — Flensburg
   Mar. 17, 1879 — Steglitz near Berlin

Franz G. L. Struve: unknown; farmer, U. S. consul general.
   1809 — Oldenburg, Prussia
   June 30, 1874 — Quebec, Canada

Henry Tigler: university student, later brewery owner; distillery
   owner.
   Unknown
   Unknown, presumed Osnabrück, Germany

L. H. Trayser: cabinetmaker; cabinetmaker, furniture dealer.
   1826 — Hesse
   Feb. 1898 — Waterloo, Wisconsin

William Wiggenhorn: merchant, postmaster; hotel owner.
   Apr. 23, 1797 — Westphalia
   Dec. 12, 1876 — Watertown

Hermann H. Winter: university student; farmer, politics.
   1805 — Hannover
   Sept. 28, 1884 — Watertown

SELECTED BIBLIOGRAPHY AND OTHER SOURCES

Blumenfeld, Ralph D. *Home Town*. London: Hutchinson & Co., (Publishers) Ltd., 1944.

Colonius, H. C. "Geschichte von Watertown, nach mündlichen Überlieferungen," serially in *Watertown Weltbürger* beginning Sept. 26, 1868; repeated serially in same paper beginning Apr. 15, 1905.

Cooper, Berenice. "Die Freien Gemeinden in Wisconsin." Transactions of the Wisconsin Academy of Sciences, Arts, and Letters, Vol. 53 (1964).

Easum, Chester Verne. *The Americanization of Carl Schurz*. Chicago: University of Chicago Press, 1929.

Feuss, Claude Moore. *Carl Schurz, Reformer*. New York: Dodd, Mead & Company, 1932.

Gaebler, Max H. and Gaebler, Hans D. "William C. Chappell and His Times, Stories of Old Watertown, Wisconsin." n.p., n.d. Six typewritten essays. Watertown Historical Society collection, No. 5218.

Hamerow, Theodore S. *Restoration, Revolution, Reaction*. Princeton, New Jersey: Princeton University Press. First Princeton Paperback Edition, Fourth Printing, 1972.

History of Jefferson County, Wisconsin. Chicago: Western Historical Company, 1879.

Jacobi, C. Hugo. "Reminiscences of Early Days in Watertown." Serially in *Watertown Daily Times*, beginning Feb. 1, 1924 (original articles in German in *Watertown Weltbürger* beginning May 5, 1923). The July 7, 1923 German article was omitted in the English reprint of 1924. It was translated and printed in the *Daily Times* beginning Nov. 3, 1986. English and German versions of the entire series are not identical; English version is more detailed and was used in preparing this material.

Kiessling, Elmer C. *Watertown Remembered*. Watertown: Franklin Publishers Incorporated for the Watertown Historical Society, 1976.

Marquardt, Ralph. Former president of the Free Congregation of Sauk City, Wis., and authority on the free religious movement. Personal interview, Prairie du Sac, Wisconsin, July 12, 1989.

Oehlerts, Donald E. *Guide to Wisconsin Newspapers 1833-1957*. Madison: State Historical Society of Wisconsin, 1958.

Ott, John Henry, ed. *Jefferson County, Wisconsin and Its People*, 2 vols. Chicago: S. J. Clarke Publishing Company, 1917.

Rippley, La Vern J. *The German Americans*. Lanham, Maryland: University Press of America, 1976.

Rippley, La Vern J. *The Immigrant Experience in Wisconsin*. Boston: Twayne Publishers, 1985.

Schafer, Joseph, trans. and ed. *Intimate Letters of Carl Schurz*. Madison, Wisconsin: State Historical Society of Wisconsin, 1929.

Schurz, Carl. *The Reminiscences of Carl Schurz*. New York: McClure Press, 1907.

Trefousse, Hans L. *Carl Schurz*. Knoxville, Tennessee: University of Tennessee Press, 1982.

Wallman, Charles J. *Edward J. Brandt, Inventor*. Watertown, Wisconsin: Brandt, Inc., 1984.

Whyte, William F. "Beginnings of the Watertown School System." Wisconsin Magazine of History, Sept. 1923.

Whyte, William F. "Bennett Law Campaign in Wisconsin." Wisconsin Magazine of History, Mar. 1923.

Whyte, William F. "Chronicles of Early Watertown." Wisconsin Magazine of History, Mar. 1921.

Whyte, William F. "Settlement of the Town of Lebanon, Dodge County." Proceedings of the Society at its Sixty-Third

Annual Meeting held Oct. 21, 1915. Published by the Society, 1916.

Whyte, William F. "Watertown Railway Bond Fight." Proceedings of the Society at its Sixty-Fourth Annual Meeting held Oct. 19, 1916. Published by the Society in Madison, 1917.

Wittke, Carl. *The German-American Press in America.* New York: Haskell House Publishers Ltd., 1973.

Wittke, Carl. *Refugees of Revolution.* Philadelphia: University of Pennsylvania Press, 1952.

Zucker, A. E. *The Forty-Eighters.* New York: Columbia University Press, 1950.

In May 1936 an article appeared in the *Milwaukee* (Wisconsin) *Journal* under the title "Watertown, Wis., Rich in Traditions of Forty-Eighters." A clipping of the article is on file at the Watertown Public Library and bears the identification 977.58/Z3. Repeated attempts have failed to determine its exact date of publication.

NEWSPAPERS AND DIRECTORIES

Harger Times. Watertown, Wisconsin. (Jan. 5, 1878-Sept. 7, 1878)

Rock River Pilot. Watertown, Wisconsin. (Oct. 13, 1847-Oct. 4, 1848).

Watertown Anzeiger. Watertown, Wisconsin. (Aug. 27, 1853-Feb. 24, 1855).

Watertown Chronicle. Watertown, Wisconsin. (June 23, 1847-Oct. 11, 1854).

Watertown City Directory for 1872. Compiled and Published by Carl F. Herrmann. Watertown: J. H. Keyes, Republican Job Printing Office, 1872.

Watertown Daily Times. Watertown, Wisconsin. (Jan. 2, 1897-present).

Watertown Democrat. Watertown, Wisconsin. (Oct. 26, 1854-Feb. 22, 1883).

Watertown Gazette. Watertown, Wisconsin. (July 22, 1879-Mar. 18, 1937).

Watertown Directory, City Record and Advertiser for 1866-67. Watertown: D. W. Ballou, Publisher, 1866.

Watertown Register. Watertown, Wisconsin. (Mar. 12, 1850-Nov. 4, 1854).

Watertown Republican. Watertown, Wisconsin. (Apr. 24., 1867-Apr. 6, 1906).

Watertown Weltbürger. Watertown, Wisconsin. Name also appears as *Der Weltbürger, Weltbürger, Der Weltbürger und Anzeiger.* (Aug. 4, 1860-Dec. 2, 1932).

INDEX

NOTE: The names of individuals who are cited in this narrative as having been part of the Watertown community, but who were not part of the 1848-49 revolutions, are marked in this index with an asterisk (*)

The Author

Charles J. Wallman was born in Kiel, Wisconsin, and has been a resident of Watertown, Wisconsin, since early youth. He attended Marquette University, the University of Texas-El Paso, and the University of Wisconsin-Madison from which he graduated with a B. B. A.

From 1948 until 1983 he served in various capacities with Brandt, Inc., in Watertown and retired in 1983 as Vice President-Corporate Development. He had also been a director of the firm. Mr. Wallman's numerous professional and civic contributions are recognized in *Who's Who in the Midwest, Who's Who in Finance and Industry,* and *Who's Who in the World.*

The author's first direct involvement with Germany was in World War II, both as a soldier and as a prisoner of war in Germany. His command of the German language and his interest in local history led him gradually to study the German tradition of Watertown, Wisconsin. This city owed its thriving cultural life in the mid and late 19th century in great part to its German-speaking immigrants. For a time it was the second largest city in Wisconsin. The founder of the company with which Mr. Wallman had been associated was the son of one of the German revolutionaries of 1848 and had been connected professionally with Richard Wagner in Dresden. Educational history had been made in Watertown when America's first kindergarten classses were introduced.

A long-time and dedicated study of newspaper archives, city documents, many personal connections with Watertown residents, and an interest in social history have resulted in numerous articles and lectures on the German-Americans of Watertown. Mr. Wallman's book *Edward J. Brandt, Inventor,* appeared in 1984.

Mr. Wallman has been an active alumnus of the University of Wisconsin-Madison. In his retirement he has shared his knowledge and enthusiasm with faculty, students, and interested visitors from the United States and German-speaking countries of Europe.

Mr. Wallman is married to the former Charline M. Moore. He has five children and several grandchildren.